ENJOYING

BOURBON

© 2021 Quarto Publishing Group USA Inc.

First Published in 2021 by Voyageur Press, an imprint of The Quarto Group, 100 Cummings Center, Suite 265-D, Beverly, MA 01915, USA. T (978) 282-9590 F (978) 283-2742 QuartoKnows.com

Voyageur Press titles are also available at discount for retail, wholesale, promotional, and bulk purchase. For details, contact the Special Sales Manager by email at specialsales@quarto.com or by mail at The Quarto Group, Attn: Special Sales Manager, 100 Cummings Center, Suite 265-D, Beverly, MA 01915, USA.

25 24 23 22 21   1 2 3 4 5

ISBN: 978-0-7603-6926-5

Digital edition published in 2021
eISBN: 978-0-7603-6927-2

Library of Congress Control Number: 2021939528

Design and Page Layout: Ashley Prine, Tandem Books
Cover Frame: Vasya Kobelev/Shutterstock
Cover Illustration: NataLima/Shutterstock
Interior Illustrations and Photography: See page 176

Printed in China

ENJOYING

BOURBON

A TASTING GUIDE AND JOURNAL

FRANK FLANNERY

VOYAGEUR
PRESS

CONTENTS

TASTING NOTES

INTRODUCTION

Welcome to *Enjoying Bourbon: A Tasting Guide and Journal*. On these pages you'll learn everything you need to know to appreciate this distinctly American whiskey for all its depth and character. Originally from the farmlands of Kentucky, bourbon has been a national favorite pretty much since America became a nation. In the centuries since, the honored traditions of using corn mash and charred oak barrels—the process that makes bourbon bourbon— has led to the creation of some of the finest whiskey in the world.

This book explores the history of bourbon, from its colonial roots in necessity to its modern status as esteemed native spirit. Find out how bourbon is made and what's changed about the process over these past couple hundred years (spoiler: the truth is "not too much"). Get answers to the big bourbon questions, like "Does bourbon have to be made in Kentucky?" and "What's the difference between bourbon and other kinds of whiskey?"

You'll also learn how to read a bourbon label like a true aficionado, so you can tell what you're getting before you buy a bottle. What's legalese, what's marketing, and what's actually important will all be explained. Then the best part: really tasting bourbon. Find out what the experts pay attention to when they're drinking bourbon so that you get the most from every sip as you fill out the journal pages with your own tasting notes. From the look and the smell to the taste and the linger, every bourbon has its own story to tell. You just need to know how to listen.

Finally, you'll visit some of America's leading bourbon producers to see what makes them so popular. If you taste along with the notes in this book, you'll really get a baseline for bourbon sipping that will help you fill in your own tasting notes with satisfaction and ease. I hope you enjoy your journey into the oaky world of America's native spirit!

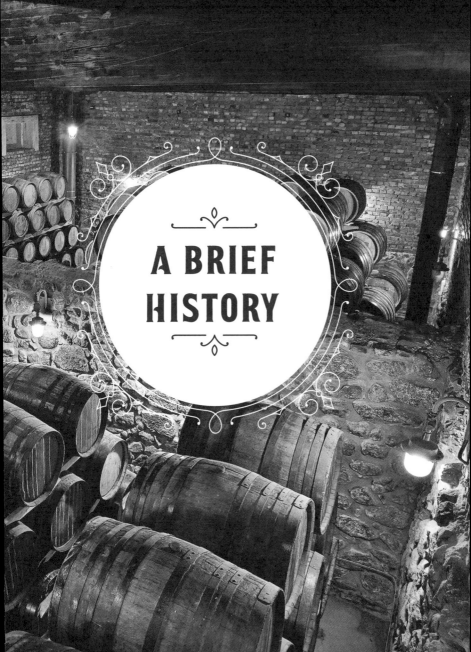

A BRIEF
HISTORY

THE SPIRIT OF A NEW NATION

Bourbon's history is an American history, with its creation tied in with the birth of the nation. One of the first things the colonies made was alcohol by using their excess crops—when there were any. In a time when safe drinking water wasn't as easy as turning on a faucet, beer and ciders were important for hydration and even nutrition. In terms of spirits, which were also important in colonial life, rum was the most popular in the early days because it could be made cheaply using molasses imported from the East Indies. After the first Americans threw off British rule in the Revolutionary War, though, cheap sugar went with the tyranny. Breaking up with Britain meant that, among many changes, newly minted Americans had to turn to native grains to make their liquor.

As the war came to a close in the late 1700s, pioneers from Scotland, Ireland, England, Germany, and France began settling areas west of the Appalachian Mountains, including a sprawling and fertile area that was established as Bourbon County in 1785. Originally part of the state of Virginia, it was named for the French royal House of Bourbon, which had supported the revolutionaries in the war. In 1792, Bourbon and surrounding counties officially separated from Virginia to form the state of Kentucky. European settlers in the area had brought with them distilling techniques from their home countries, and as they farmed the area, they also distilled spirits using the grains they were growing, including maize, also known then as Indian corn.

And that's pretty much all the general history everyone can agree on. After that, the details of how the all the methods used on individual farm distilleries turned into the purposeful, specific method of making corn-based whiskey in charred oak barrels that makes bourbon bourbon are a bit like the morning after a night at

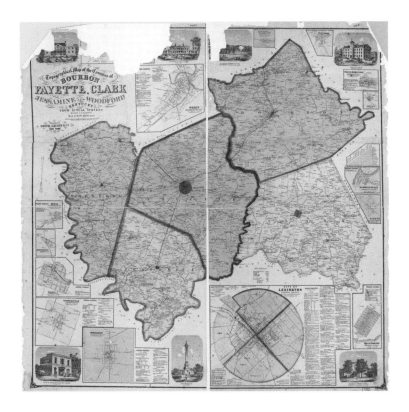

the bar—a little fuzzy. For instance, the first commercial distillery to allegedly open in the area that would become Louisville, Kentucky, was said to have been started by Welsh immigrant Evan Williams in 1783, back when Kentucky was just a county in Virginia. Some historians contest these claims, but "Since 1783" still appears on modern bottles of Evan Williams, which in itself is a little confusing since the distillery producing that bourbon today does not have a direct connection to the one purportedly opened back in the eighteenth century. Another example of the murky details is the story that Elijah Craig invented bourbon as we know it in 1789, though there isn't any evidence to back that up and the story didn't start appearing in print until 1874.

BUT IS IT "BOURBON"?

The earliest reference to "Bourbon Whiskey" we have is an advertisement from the merchants Stout and Adams that dates back to 1821. It's unknown if the liquor being advertised is in fact the kind of whiskey that came to be known as bourbon. The term was most likely used just to indicate that the whiskey was from the area called Bourbon, which was almost certainly known for its corn whiskey at that point, but was it always aged in charred oak barrels (a very necessary element of distilling bourbon)? Maybe but definitely not certainly. Charring barrels was a common practice to get rid of the taste of whatever had been previously stored in the barrels. It would neutralize the old

ANOTHER ETYMOLOGY

While most people agree that bourbon is so called for the county that famously produces it, there are others, namely historian Michael Veach, who say it was named for Bourbon Street in New Orleans, Louisiana, a port and party town where a lot of Kentucky whiskey was imbibed. The argument goes that "bourbon" began appearing on labels in the 1850s, but people didn't start attributing that to Bourbon County until the 1870s. Veach believes that it was called bourbon long before that because people wanted the whiskey sold on Bourbon Street and that eventually just got shortened to bourbon. The whole Bourbon County thing, which was certainly not the only county producing bourbon, was just a coincidence that led to confusion down the timeline.

flavor, but whatever was next stored in the barrels took on a bit of that charred flavor. The first mention we have of using such barrels for aging—a definitive aspect of making bourbon—goes back to 1826, when a grocer in Lexington, Kentucky, asked distiller John Corliss specifically for that kind of whiskey. Corn whiskey aged in charred oak barrels was sure to have a distinct and probably more pleasing flavor than a lot of the other spirits on the market at that time, and it was well on its way to becoming a distinct commodity.

Through the nineteenth century, distilling techniques were written down and refined. These may seem like super-obvious things to do, but a formalized scientific method was kind of new back then. As hard as it is to imagine, experimenting on a recipe in a purposeful way and writing down your results was itself an innovation. So when Dr. James C. Crow, a Scottish immigrant with a background in not just medicine but also chemistry, began working for Glenns Creek Distillery in Woodford County,

Kentucky, in 1835, and refined the sour mash process using the newfangled scientific method, it was a game changer. He perfected putting already fermented mash into unfermented mash to make a fully fermented mash to use in the distillation. Because he wrote it all down precisely, he could therefore repeat the process to create more reliable libations.

That wasn't the only game changer at the time, however. Aeneas Coffey invented the column still in the 1830s, a technology that allowed for distilleries to grow as the spreading rail lines increased distribution potential and therefore demand.

GETTING IN THE MIDDLE

At this time, bourbon was mostly sold in barrels to grocers and saloons. People would then come with bottles in hand to fill up. The only problem was the middlemen. Rectifiers, as they were called, would buy barrels from distilleries and then dilute them

LONG TRADITIONS

Among the arguments over the who and what of bourbon history are the various claims about which Kentucky distillery is the oldest. Some believe Buffalo Trace, founded in 1792, is the oldest continually operational distillery, though construction of its first distillery wasn't recorded until 1812. Burks Distillery, which opened in 1805 and today produces Maker's Mark (its bonded warehouse is shown opposite), is recognized by the *Guinness Book of World Records* as the oldest bourbon distillery. Jim Beam says it started selling bourbon in 1795, calling it Old Jake Beam Sour Mash. And then there's the story that the Baptist preacher Elijah Craig "invented" bourbon by letting corn whiskey, which was already popular, age. Almost all agree that bourbon developed regionally and was not invented per se, but Craig did open a distillery in 1789.

using water, neutral spirits, and other flavoring and coloring ingredients. Glass bottles were becoming easier and cheaper to manufacture, and people began buying bottles of alcohol labeled "bourbon," a term that had prestige by now, but was watered down or otherwise adulterated and was a far cry from the actual bourbon that distillers were working so hard to create. Needless to say, the distillers and the consumers were getting a little . . . disgruntled about the situation.

This literal watering down led to some of the first consumer-protection legislation in the United States. First the Bottled-in-Bond Act of 1897 allowed distillers to age their bourbon in a bonded government warehouse. The bourbon was then proofed down, bottled, and given clear labeling and a federal strip stamp that guaranteed consumers were getting the bourbon they thought they were getting, instead of some neutral spirit flavored with

tobacco and prune juice. Using bonded warehouses also meant distillers had to pay tax only on bottles that left the warehouse— not earlier in the process, when they might be taxed on product they ended up having to scrap for any reason.

Now distillers and consumers were happy but rectifiers were not, and they challenged the act in court. Meanwhile, the Pure Food and Drug Act passed in 1906, which legislated more truth in labeling including and beyond alcohol. Bottles could not be labeled "pure whiskey," but it wasn't until the 1909 Taft Decision that the term was actually defined. The Taft Decision created three categories of whiskey: straight, blended, and imitation. It also required straight bourbon to be distilled from at least 51 percent corn, to be aged in charred oak barrels for two years, and to be bottled at less than 62.5 percent alcohol by volume.

UPS AND DOWNS AND UPS AGAIN

It would seem like a new, bright day was dawning for distillers and drinkers alike, but in fact the temperance movement was ramping up and the United States would soon get involved in World War I. During the war, distilleries focused on making neutral spirits for ammunition, and then shortly after the war ended, Prohibition began. For thirteen years, the only alcohol legally available and produced in America was for "medicinal" purposes. By the time that mess was over, the country was in the Great Depression. New alcohol regulations were passed, including one important one for bourbon: It had to be aged in *new* charred oak barrels. Presumably this was to help make jobs for coopers.

World War II came, and distillers again got in the munitions game, but after the war, the American economy boomed. The 1950s and '60s saw growth across loads of industries, including bourbon production. In fact, in 1964, Congress declared bourbon

ONLY IN AMERICA

Many people think bourbon has to come from Kentucky, but in fact the only legal geographic requirement for the native spirit is that it be made in the United States. Today there are roughly two thousand whiskey distilleries spread out across all fifty states, and many of them have a hand in the bourbon game.

was "a distinctive product of the United States," much as champagne can really only be produced in the Champagne region of France and whisky (note the lack of "e") can be called Scotch only if it's from Scotland. This congressional resolution, however, did not reflect bourbon's popularity. Americans at the time were gravitating toward lighter-style whiskeys and clear alcohols. Bourbon was seen as old fashioned, out of style, something your grandfather drank.

Distillers were sitting on barrels they couldn't sell, and in the 1980s they started marketing special-edition bottles aged for twelve years or fifteen years, trying to spin their age as a selling point, and indeed the flavors did deepen and arguably improve with age. It wasn't until the turn of the twenty-first century, however, that bourbon really came back into style. Mixology and classic cocktails became massively popular, and bourbon production rose to meet the needs of a new generation of discerning drinkers. Small-batch bourbons became and remain popular, and distilleries have popped up all around the country, creating bourbons with an incredible range of profiles at pretty much any price you want—or are willing—to pay.

✳ ✳ ✳

MAKING
BOURBON

GRAINS, MILLS, AND MASH

The flavors, the colors, the aromas, the mouthfeel, the viscosity, the finish, the very feel that you get from every glass of bourbon starts with the all-mighty grains. Bourbon, as we know, must be made from at least 51 percent corn, but the other 49 percent is distiller's choice so long as it's also grain. Every distillery has its own recipe, known as the mash bill, and typically corn makes up between 60 and 80 percent of it. Rye and malted barley are popular choices for the remainder of the bill, but sometimes a distiller will go all corn, throw in some wheat, or pick an offbeat grain like quinoa. Is the road less traveled worth the trip? Only you can say.

The individual grain types, whatever they may be, are crushed and then ground into a fine flour, a process known as milling. The milled corn is cooked in water, and as the cooking temperature is lowered, the other grains as well as some previously fermented mash are added in—this is the sour mash process developed by Dr. James C. Crow. The water itself makes up the majority of what ends up in the bottle, so common tap won't do. Kentucky's bedrock is mostly limestone, which is great at filtering. Many distilleries are located on natural springs and use that lovely, clear water to make their bourbon. Distilleries that don't have spring water have to treat the water they use to remove minerals that can affect the taste of the bourbon. The cooking process releases starch from the corn and enzymes from the grain. The enzymes break down the starch into the sugars needed for fermentation. The cooked mash is cooled and fermented in tanks using yeast.

EVERYTHING MATTERS

The grains, their ratios, the water, the sour mash, the yeast, and the material the fermentation tanks are made from are all carefully developed by distillers, as each element in the production process has an impact on the profile of their bourbon. While bourbon used to be made from leftover grain, those ingredients are now carefully selected and used in precise ratios per the distillery's mash bill. The mineral content in the water is studied. Yeast strains are vigilantly cultured. The fermentation tanks are constructed from well-considered materials ranging from metal to aged wood. Every step and every element that goes into those steps is important and perfected.

FERMENTATION AND DISTILLATION

In the tanks, the mash bubbles away for several days as the yeast converts the sugar into alcohol and releases carbon dioxide. The thick liquid produced from the fermentation process is called "distiller's beer" or "wash." The fermented mash is then pumped into a column still (there are a few distillers that use other kinds of stills, but the column still allows for continuous production and is therefore popular for anyone looking to make a good amount of bourbon). The still boils off the alcohol, which rises to the top of the still as a vapor. The water and leftover grain material collects at the bottom, some of which is used again in the sour mash process. The alcoholic vapor rises and condenses into liquid at the top of the still, where it is collected. The resulting alcohol is then redistilled in a doubler, which is a copper pot still. The alcohol from this second distillation is a

clear liquid, often called "white dog," that is usually between 65 and 80 percent alcohol by volume (abv), or 130 to 160 proof. Water is added to bring the white dog down to at least 62.5 percent abv, or 125 proof, the legal maximum alcohol content that bourbon can be stored at.

AGING

The white dog is then aged in new but charred oak barrels. The barrels are stored in warehouses, also called rickhouses, for as long as the producer wants. There is no minimum aging requirements by law, and producers age their bourbons for as little as three months; however, most bourbons are aged for years. The warehouses are climate-controlled, but there are temperature variations throughout the building. Barrels are often moved around so that they age at different temperatures at different stages of their development. As the alcohol ages, it picks up flavors from the wood and char. It also oxidizes, which breaks down some of the harsher alcohol notes. This barrel aging is the most consequential part of the process, as it has the biggest effect on the character of the bourbon. This is when bourbon gets its distinctive color and flavor.

IT'S ALL ABOUT THE BARREL

Bourbon barrels must be new and they must be made of oak. American white oak grows in abundance in the Ozark Mountains, so it's a popular choice, but any oak can technically be used. Oak logs are cut into staves, the slats that barrels are constructed out of, and the best ones are yard seasoned, meaning they're left to sit out in a lumberyard to, no joke, grow some mold. There they are also subjected to rain, sun, heat, humidity, and whatever else Mother Nature decides to do. Microorganisms grow and tiny cracks form, which the alcohol will seep into during aging, deepening the bourbon's flavor and color.

After the staves are seasoned for one to three years, coopers fashion them into barrels, strapping them together with metal bands. Most barrels hold 53 gallons, though there is no regulation size. The empty barrels are then put over a fire so that their insides can char. Charring the oak caramelizes sugars from the wood, which gives bourbon its sweetness. The char also acts as a filter during aging as the alcohol seeps into the tiny fissures in the wood. The barrels are therefore hugely important as they give bourbon its color and much of its flavor.

FROM BARREL TO BOTTLE

Producers may choose to vat the bourbon, meaning they mix barrels of different ages to create a specific flavor they're after. They can also choose to filter the bourbon using charcoal or a chill filtration process that removes fatty acids from the bourbon, or they can skip filtering and move on to proofing. Proofing is the process of slowly adding pure water to bring the abv down to a minimum of 40 percent, or 80 proof, though most producers usually don't go that low. The bourbon is then bottled and rested before being labeled and shipped to your favorite stores and bars.

✳ ✳ ✳

READING
A LABEL

DEFINING BOURBON

Along with its rich history and distilling traditions, the term "bourbon" brings a very specific spirit to the table. For starters, bourbon is, of course, a type of whiskey, and whiskey is defined, in part, as a spirit distilled from a fermented mash of grains and bottled at at least 80 proof. For a whiskey to be labeled "bourbon" in the United States, it has to meet a strict list of requirements beyond that. To start, it has to be produced in the United States. Kentucky is bourbon's original home and most bottles you find continue to be produced there, but bourbon can be distilled in any of the fifty states.

To properly be called bourbon, a spirit must also be made of a mash that is at least 51 percent corn, which in this context is considered a grain. (It can also be considered a fruit. Who knew?) Bourbon can be made from 100 percent corn, though that usually isn't the case. The recipe for the remaining 49 percent of

BOTTLED-IN-BOND

Some of the US regulations for calling a bourbon "bottled-in-bond" go all the way back to the Bottled-in-Bond Act of 1897 (see page 15). To earn the right to use this distinguished term, and the higher price tag it usually demands, distillers must fill the bottle with a bourbon that was distilled at one distillery during one season (spring being January to June and fall being July to December) and then aged in a federally bonded warehouse for at least four years. Bottled-in-bond bourbons must also be exactly 100 proof, or 50 percent abv.

the mash varies widely from distiller to distiller, but it must be made from other grains, the list of which used to be limited to the traditional cereal grains: corn, wheat, rye, and barley. But we are living in the heyday of small-batch and small-scale with distillers eager to try new things and stand out in the market. In December 2018 the Treasury Department's Tobacco Tax and Trade Bureau (TTB) expanded its list of acceptable whiskey grains to include "pseudocereal" grains such as quinoa, buckwheat, and amaranth.

The fermented, predominantly corn grain mash must then be distilled so that it is at most 160 proof, or 80 percent alcohol by volume (abv). It must then be aged at no more than 125 proof, or 62.5 percent abv, so it can be watered down a titch before barreling and aging. To put "bourbon" on the bottle, that aging has to take place in *new* charred oak barrels. This wasn't always the case, as charring barrels was a way to neutralize a barrel so that it could be used again to transport different goods, but the modern legal definition requires the aging barrels to be new. (Go back to the history on page 17 to find out why.) Aging time is totally up to the distiller, but typically it takes three months at the very least. If a distiller wants to label its whiskey as "straight bourbon," it has to let it age for at least two years, and if it's aged for less than four, this must be stated on the label.

Finally, bourbon must be bottled at no lower than 80 proof, or 40 percent abv, which means diluting the alcohol with pure water. And that's the *only* thing distillers can add to bourbon and still call it bourbon. Unlike other types of whiskeys, no colorings, flavorings, or other additives and other spirits can be added to bourbon.

These are the rules for bourbon in the United States. Canada follows the US standards but the farther you get from bourbon's Kentucky home, the looser the guidelines for what producers can label as bourbon. While most countries around the world agree that to call a spirit "bourbon," it must at least be produced in the United States, they by no means require a spirit to follow the regulations that the US has put in place to use that word on a label.

NAVIGATING A BOURBON LABEL

Depending on the bottle, a bourbon label might tell you a whole lot or very little. Some of that text is straightforward, federally regulated information that tells you very specific facts about the bourbon, whereas some of it is just marketing copy that tells you a pretty story about nothing much at all. The rule of thumb is that if a producer is proud of their process, they're going to want to tell you about it in no uncertain terms, though probably not at great length. If the text you find is vague and you don't really know what they're getting at, know that it's not your fault. They likely worked at being alluring yet evasive. Here's what you need to know to see the truth.

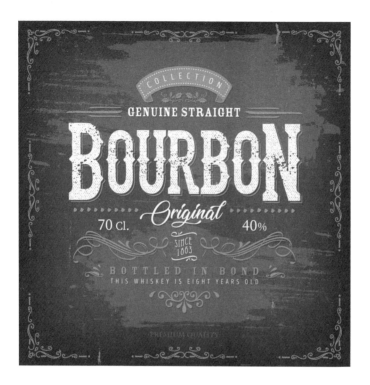

The Brand, the Company, the Distiller

The biggest, boldest thing you'll see on most bourbon labels, or any bottle label for that matter, is the name of the brand. "Brand," however, is not necessarily synonymous with the company that bottled the bourbon or with the distiller. A bourbon may be branded with one name by a company that buys bourbon from one or more distillers. Or a distiller may be also be the company and the brand name. This information can be divined, to some degree, on the label.

The TTB requires a label to tell you what company bottled a spirit using language like "bottled by," "crafted by," or even "made by," but unless the label says "distilled by" or "distilled and bottled by," you're getting the name of the company that bottled the bourbon and not the name of the distiller. Not that that's a bad thing. Lots of truly excellent bourbons are bottled by a company that works with a distiller or number of distillers to make small batches, higher proofs, or otherwise specialized runs of bourbon. The labels for domestic spirits all require an address, meaning just city and state, but that address can be that of the bottler or the producer or the distiller or the parent company, meaning that it doesn't tell you much about where the spirit was actually distilled, but fortunately . . .

The Where

Another legal requirement for bourbon labels is that they give the name of the state where it was distilled. More often than not, that state is Kentucky and you'll see that printed in pride of place on the front label, maybe with city or town name added in to give off more small-batch vibe. Other times you'll have to go to the back of the bottle to find where the bourbon was distilled, and if you have to do that, odds are you won't see "Kentucky" printed there. Again, that's not a bad thing. Kentucky is the birthplace and a lot of people strongly associate bourbon with that state, but fine bourbons are increasingly being produced outside this spirit's ancestral home.

The Age

US law also requires the label to state a bourbon's age if it is younger than four years old. That age is determined by how long the bourbon was aged in the barrel, not the bottle, and by the *youngest* bourbon in the bottle. A label doesn't have to give the bourbon's age if it is a straight bourbon, which by definition is

aged for at least two years, or a bottled-in-bond bourbon, which has to be aged for at least four. A lot of producers decide to include the age as a point of pride, but ages in general are starting to disappear from labels, and when they do show up, often the wording is not exactly concrete. While you can enjoy a bourbon regardless of its age, know that labels that say things like "aged less than four years" or something otherwise nonspecific are being a little cagey about their age. You can judge for yourself why that might be and if it even matters.

* * *

TASTING
BOURBON

BEFORE YOU POUR

That tawny look, that alcohol-rich aroma, that warm feeling as it spreads across your tongue. Tasting bourbon is a lush indulgence that deepens with experience and expertise. As with fine wine and food, there is an art to tasting bourbon that will help you savor each encounter and get the most out of every tasting. And it starts before you even put your hands on the bottle. When you want to taste a bourbon—really explore it for its qualities both bold and subtle—there are a few things you can do to ensure the best experience possible.

Glassware

People who take their bourbon seriously almost always reach for a Glencairn glass when they're conducting a tasting. These Scottish crystal glasses are the product of decades of development, industry infighting, and ultimately cooperation, all aimed at coming up with

a glass that is perfect for tasting whiskey. While they do make for a nice experience, you certainly don't have to use them to have a quality tasting. The advantages of these tulip-shaped tasting glasses are that they aren't too big, they allow you to swirl the whiskey without spilling it, and you can get your nose in there so that you can get a good whiff. As long as you choose a glass that fits that bill, you'll have a good experience. A snifter, a small wine glass, or even a rocks glass will do nicely.

Serving

A little goes a long way in a bourbon tasting. You need only about half an ounce, or a tablespoon to put it in more visual terms, to get a thorough taste of a bourbon. This is especially true if you plan on tasting a flight (a sampling of usually three or more bourbons). The more you drink, the duller your senses, so if you're serious about tasting the bourbon for all it's worth instead of all its effects, stick to small amounts. And it likely goes without saying, but bourbon should be served at room temperature.

It's also a good idea to have some spring water on hand, which you can add to the bourbon to open up the flavors. It's also good to have spring or sparkling water on hand to keep hydrated and cleanse your palate. Unsalted crackers, popcorn, or bread also works as palate cleansers. You can also try doing some food pairings with your bourbon. Sharp cheeses, dark chocolate, toasted nuts, and dried dark fruit all go very well with bourbon; but if you're serious about tasting several bourbons, be sure to cleanse those strong

flavors from your palate before moving on to the next bottle. You also don't want to start tasting while hungry or very full. Eat a little while beforehand so that you're sated but not stuffed.

BEFORE YOU SIP
After you've poured your bourbon, or bourbons, take a moment to observe the spirit before you begin to sip it.

The Color
A bourbon's color can tell you something about what

to expect from the spirit itself. The darker the color, the longer the bourbon was likely barrel aged, which usually also indicates a higher proof. It could also indicate how charred the barrel was, which will have a distinct effect on the spirit's flavor. If the bourbon is cloudy, that probably means it was not filtered to remove the fatty acids that built up during aging.

Whiskey Tears

If you swirl the bourbon in the glass, this does two things. First, it'll show you the bourbon's "tears," the slow trails of spirit that run down the side of the glass after a swirl or a sip. (In wine and for other spirits, this is often referred to as the "legs.") Typically, the slower the tears, the higher the alcohol content. As tempting as it is to use this as an indicator of quality,  it's just an effect of the abv, nothing more. Second, and more important, this little bit of aeration will allow a bit of the alcohol to evaporate and thus open up the more subtle smells so that you can get a good whiff.

The Nose

Since bourbon is high in alcohol, you'll want to bring it to your nose slowly. This will let your nose acclimate to the alcohol and smell the bourbon's real aroma. Hold the glass under your nose

until you get used to the astringency of the alcohol, and then take a more considered sniff. You can pass the glass back and forth under your nose, you can dip your nose into the glass, or you can take long, slow sniffs. There are experts that make arguments for all these styles and more, so just remember that everyone's nose is different, and your nose knows what's right for you.

As you take in the aroma, also called the "nose," try to discern different notes. You'll likely first get sweet notes of caramel or vanilla, but if you take your time, you're likely to discover more, including:

Sweet
caramel/toffee
vanilla
honey
maple syrup
chocolate

Fruity and Floral
apple
pear
cherry
berry
dark fruit
lemon
orange
grapefruit
rose
honeysuckle
lilac

Spicy and Herbal
black pepper
tobacco
cloves
cinnamon sticks
mint
licorice
ginger

Woody and Nutty
oak
cedar
pine
sawdust
coffee
charcoal smoke
almond
pecan
hazelnut
walnut

TASTING

You've already had quite a detailed sensory experience with your bourbon, and you haven't even taken your first sip yet. But you are primed to get the most out of every drop. Keep in mind the color and the notes you picked up on the nose as you begin to slowly imbibe your bourbon.

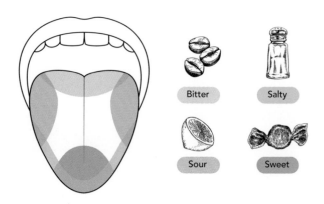

The First Sip

Your first sip, and I do mean sip and not shot, should be enough to allow you to roll the bourbon around in your mouth, covering all the different parts of your tongue. Different regions of the tongue detect different flavors, so you'll want to make sure the bourbon passes over your whole tongue so that you get the whole flavor. Try to discern some of the individual flavors. Do you notice some of the flavors you detected on the nose in your mouth?

Don't be surprised if on the first sip you don't get much distinction between flavors. Bourbon is a strong spirit, and it will take your taste buds a little bit of time to acclimate to the alcohol and then sense past it to detect the subtler flavors.

The Third Sip

By the third sip, you should be able to better pick up on the different flavors that underlie the alcohol. You may find the same ones you detected on the nose, or you might find new ones entirely. Some experts would urge you to make an O with your mouth and breathe in some air while swishing the bourbon in your mouth, essentially gargling it, while others will tell you that's silly. You do you. As long as you take your time and make sure bourbon hits each part of your tongue and mouth, you'll get a full picture of its flavor. As you do this, you'll also be experiencing the body of the whiskey, or how it feels in your mouth. Usually this is described from light to heavy, but some whiskey pros also put viscosity and heat in the body category.

WHAT ABOUT WATER?

There are some experts who believe whiskey should be tasted neat, with no water or ice added, if you want to experience its truest flavor. Increasingly, however, people recommend adding a few drops of water before the second or third sip, or even later, to lower the alcohol content and open up the aroma and flavor. Do your best to get a neutral water, maybe distilled or at least bottled, so that you're not affecting the taste of the bourbon with your chlorine-heavy tap water, for example.

You can buy a fancy pipette for this, or just use a straw and cap one end with a finger to mete out drops of water. Just a few drops should do it, but you're the ultimate judge. The same holds true for putting in ice. There are some whiskey pros who look down their noses at putting a cube of ice in a bourbon during a tasting, saying it locks up the flavors, but if you try it and like it, that's the only thing that counts.

The Finish

After you've swallowed the bourbon, the last thing to notice is how your mouth feels and tastes now. Do you still taste any of the flavors? Do you perhaps taste something new? And how does your mouth feel? Perhaps it feels oily or dry or warm. Maybe a taste or sensation lingers for a long finish or just up and dissipates before you know it. If you decide to add water to your bourbon tasting, you'll likely get a different finish pre- and post-hydration. No matter how it goes, be sure to write it down.

A TASTING FLIGHT

If you're tasting a flight of bourbons, it's a good idea to go from the lowest proof to the highest, as the higher the proof, the more intense the alcohol will be. If you go big first, you'll blow out your taste

buds for the littler guys. The highest proof is likely to correspond to the lightest to darkest colors. If you start on the lower end, that will be easier on your palate and you'll be better able to taste each bourbon. That said, go slow. Enjoy yourself. There's no need to rush through the flight. Spend time with each bourbon and take a break in between to give your palate time to reset.

If possible, try doing a blind flight, where the spirit is poured for you and you don't know the brand or age of the bourbon you're tasting. This way you can experience the taste without any preconceptions. If you're doing a side-by-side comparison and don't want to let too much time pass between tasting each sample, be sure to use a palate cleanser as you switch back and forth.

* * *

FAMOUS
BOURBONS

NAMES YOU KNOW

While small-batch, local bourbons that are definitely worth your time are finding their way to shelves across the country, there are some national brands that form the limestone bedrock of the bourbon landscape. These are the big boys that you see in every store and every bar, and because they're so consistent and well known, starting your tasting journey with these can give you a solid foundation of bourbon basics.

There is, of course, near endless debate over which bourbon is the best, which expensive bottles are worth their price, and whether or not some of the most popular brands are overrated. You'll have to form your own opinions about those issues. What's presented here is the lowdown on a short list of some of the country's most popular—meaning bestselling—bourbon brands. While your personal go-to favorite might not be listed here, that just means you can start there with your own tasting notes on the journal pages that follow.

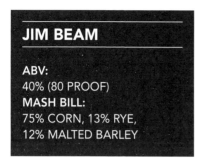

JIM BEAM

ABV:
40% (80 PROOF)
MASH BILL:
75% CORN, 13% RYE,
12% MALTED BARLEY

Jim Beam's "White Label" Kentucky Straight Bourbon Whiskey is the bestselling bourbon in the world. An eminently affordable option, its label is practically an icon of the spirit itself. With roots that can be traced back to 1795, this distillery grew from frontier beginnings to an American corporate heavyweight that then was purchased by Suntory, a Japanese food and beverage company, in 2014. Despite the changes, Jim Beam is still proudly produced in Kentucky.

Because of its immense popularity, people love to debate its quality and taste. Heated opinions aside, here are facts. While Jim Beam doesn't include an age statement on its label, online it is loud and proud about aging its "White Label" for four years, the minimum a straight bourbon must be aged without stating its age.

Its proof is as low as you can get in a bourbon, which helps smooth out this spirit.

Tasting Notes

On the lighter side of amber and sweet on the nose, you can smell the corn and oak with a bit of vanilla fruit as well. The flavor is as straightforward bourbon as it gets, with notes of caramel and vanilla. It's not as sweet as it smells, however, and you get a good amount of wood, some fruit, and possibly honey. It finishes smooth, which you'd expect from such a popular brand, and lingers for a little but not too long. This bourbon is certainly palatable for the masses and is perhaps best enjoyed in a cocktail.

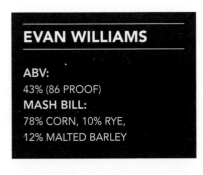

EVAN WILLIAMS

ABV:
43% (86 PROOF)
MASH BILL:
78% CORN, 10% RYE,
12% MALTED BARLEY

Made by Heaven Hill Distilleries, Evan Williams Black Kentucky Straight Bourbon Whiskey is distilled in Louisville, Kentucky, and bottled in Bardstown, about an hour away. While Evan Williams brags that it had Kentucky's first commercial distillery, historians aren't so sure. Regardless, today they make an immensely popular and well-loved bourbon. Black Label is aged four to five years, though it used to get five to seven. Enthusiasts haven't seemed to mind or notice the change, however, and this very affordable bourbon is the second bestselling in the United States.

Tasting Notes
Truly amber in color, Evan Williams Black smells of vanilla and oak with some dark caramel and dark fruit underneath. The flavor notes on the nose carry over to its taste to a large degree, though with the addition of a gingery, peppery spice and a diminishment on the oak. While not the most complex bourbon you're likely to

taste, it's solidly enjoyable with a balanced body. The finish runs medium to long, carrying the sweetness and a bit of the spice from the palate with it.

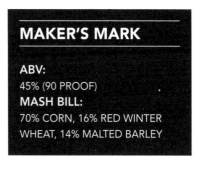

MAKER'S MARK

ABV:
45% (90 PROOF)
MASH BILL:
70% CORN, 16% RED WINTER
WHEAT, 14% MALTED BARLEY

Maker's Mark Kentucky Straight Bourbon Whiskey is a blend of handcrafted meets big business. Founded in 1953 by Bill and Margie Samuels, this brand was sold several times over the years, but the Samuels family still kept control of production until 2011. Currently owned by Beam Suntory, Maker's Mark is still handcrafted in small batches of only about nineteen barrels at a time, with those barrels hand rotated around their warehouses. Each distinctive square bottle is dipped into red wax by hand for that personal touch, but at a moderate price. Though Maker's Mark doesn't make an age statement, since it's a straight bourbon, we know it's aged for at least four years. (If it were fewer, the label would have to say so.)

Tasting Notes
The deep amber of this bourbon belies its slightly higher proof. After it's breathed for a minute, the nose is sweet with caramel, vanilla, brown sugar, syrup, and corn all arising after the initial astringency of the alcohol

evaporates. There is also oak in there and some wheat. The flavor is less sweet than the smell, but you still get the vanilla and caramel, as well as the oak, but with a bit of dark fruit to boot. Slightly on the thin side but still warming, the body makes Maker's easy to drink. It seems to finish on this side of quick, but then it comes back with some of the sweetness and vanilla, but they are dominated by an overarching dry oak.

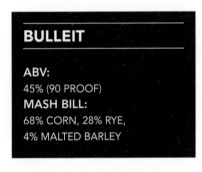

BULLEIT

ABV:
45% (90 PROOF)
MASH BILL:
68% CORN, 28% RYE,
4% MALTED BARLEY

Bulleit Kentucky Straight Bourbon bills itself as a "frontier whiskey" inspired by a recipe that pioneer Augustus Bulleit used 150 years ago. At least that's the story according to former Kentucky lawyer Tom Bulleit, Augustus's great-great-grandson. Despite this family claim to a long history, Bulleit (which, by the way, is pronounced "bull-it" like the ammo) only hit the commercial market in 1987 when Tom started producing whiskey based on his ancestor's rye-heavy recipe. In 1995, he started releasing bourbon, which, true to Bulleit form, is high on the rye. Shortly after releasing its first bottles of bourbon, the company changed hands a few times and was produced at Four Roses Distillery for a spell. Now owned by Diageo, a British food and beverage conglomerate, in March 2017 Bulleit got its very own distillery outside Shelbyville, Kentucky, with massive production capability to meet the massive demand for this popular, mid-priced brand. While Bulleit doesn't provide an age statement on its label, it

has to be aged for at least four years, meaning that the bottles produced by the Shelbyville distillery didn't start hitting shelves until spring of 2021.

Tasting Notes

This medium-amber bourbon has a sweet and spicy nose with definite notes of oak and vanilla with an astringency that is likely due to the high rye content. There is also a note of light fruit, a bit citrusy, a bit berry. The flavor is also sweet and spicy, with some toffee in it as well as baking spices and something approaching chocolate. It's got a lot of body but is still smooth and warm. You also get some oak and rye that carry through with the toffee for a long, smoky, somewhat dry finish.

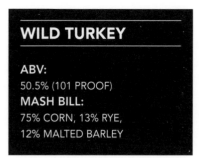

WILD TURKEY

ABV:
50.5% (101 PROOF)
MASH BILL:
75% CORN, 13% RYE,
12% MALTED BARLEY

The legend of Wild Turkey 101 Kentucky Straight Bourbon Whiskey says that an Austin Nichols executive took some bourbon samples from a distillery in Tyrone, Kentucky, on a hunting trip for wild turkey in 1940. He and his friends liked it so much that Austin Nichols started distributing it a couple years later. For the next few decades, Wild Turkey was a brand that sourced its bourbon on the open market, and while it became a favorite of legendary journalist and drinker Hunter S. Thompson, it also acquired a, shall we say, less than flattering reputation that many bourbon enthusiasts feel is entirely unfair and unfounded for the Wild Turkey of today, especially when it comes to its award-winning classic 101.

Since 1971, Wild Turkey has had its own distillery as it was bought and sold by large international beverage corporations. The Italian company Gruppo

Campari bought Wild Turkey in 2009 and invested heavily in a new distillery in Lawrenceburg, Kentucky, as well as new warehouses and a bottling plant. The brand also boasts having the longest-tenured active master distiller in Jimmy Russell, who has been in that role since the late 1960s. This mid-priced bourbon doesn't print an age statement, but it's known to be a blend of six-, seven-, and eight-year-old bourbons.

Tasting Notes

Distilled at a low proof and aged in heavily charred barrels, leather and oak come through in this dark amber bourbon. There are also notes of sweet caramel and dark fruits and berries. The flavor is a nice balance of those sweet flavors along with vanilla and spicy, oaky char. You can also taste a bit of the malt and corn and a hint of cigar. Sweetness, spice, oak, and leather dominate the long finish that has a bit of bite and dryness.

BOURBON COCKTAILS

THE MANHATTAN

Perhaps the most classic of all the whiskey recipes, the Manhattan is believed to date back to the late 1800s and is traditionally made with bourbon or rye.

2 ounces bourbon
½ ounce sweet vermouth

2 dashes bitters
cocktail cherries for garnish

Fill a mixing glass with ice. Pour in the liquid ingredients and stir until well chilled. Strain into a chilled cocktail glass. Garnish with one to three cocktail cherries.

A PERFECT VARIATION

For a slightly less sweet take on the classic Manhattan, use equal parts dry and sweet vermouth.

2 ounces bourbon
½ ounce sweet vermouth
½ ounce dry vermouth

1 dash bitters
twist of lemon or orange peel
 for garnish

Fill a mixing glass with ice. Pour in the liquid ingredients and stir until well chilled. Strain into a chilled cocktail glass. Twist your citrus peel over the drink, expressing some of the oil, and drop into the glass.

OLD-FASHIONED

This American cocktail is almost as old as bourbon itself. In the early 1800s, the word *cocktail* was just coming into use and it was essentially synonymous with this recipe. Back then you could mix any spirit with bitters, water, and sugar to make a "cocktail." Soon bartenders started making mixed drinks more complicated with a whole host of ingredients, and as cocktails got more complicated, people started asking for their drinks to be made the "old-fashioned" way when they wanted the simpler style of yesteryear. The most common way to ask for it was with whiskey. Today, an old-fashioned is made pretty much the same way it was at the start of the nineteenth century, but now it's always made with bourbon or rye.

½ teaspoon or 1 cube sugar
2 dashes Angostura bitters
1 teaspoon or 1 barspoon water
2 ounces bourbon

1 large or several small ice cubes
orange peel for garnish
maraschino cherry (optional)

In a rocks glass, muddle the sugar, bitters, and water. Add the bourbon, then the ice, and stir until well chilled. Twist the orange peel over the glass to express the oil and drop the peel into the glass. Drop in a cherry or two if you like.

MINT JULEP

The mint julep is a very old drink indeed. Southern in origin, the oldest textual reference we have to it dates to the 1770s when it (and other juleps) were used medicinally to settle an upset stomach. As ice became more widespread and popular, the mint julep got the welcome addition of crushed ice and it began to become popular as a mixed drink instead of just medicine. Today, it's perhaps most famous for its stature as the official drink of the Kentucky Derby, where revelers drink 120,000 mint juleps every year.

8–10 mint leaves (traditionally spearmint), set aside 1 for garnish

2 sugar cubes or 2 teaspoons superfine sugar
2½ ounces bourbon
crushed ice

In a julep cup, stainless steel julep cup or old-fashioned glass, muddle the mint and sugar until the mint smells strong. Pour in the bourbon, and then pack in the crushed ice. Stir until you get the cup or glass frosty. Add more crushed ice and a mint leaf for garnish.

LIQUID VARIATIONS

There are those who swear by using simple syrup instead of dry sugar. If you want to try this, you can go anywhere from ¼ ounce to 2 ounces depending on how sweet the syrup is and how sweet you like your julep. Others still will implore you to add a splash of cold water, flat or seltzer, before you put in the bourbon. All of this is right or wrong, depending on your own tastes.

HOT TODDY

Is there any better way to warm up than with a hot toddy? Though "toddy" comes to us from India by way of the British, bourbon is the perfect spirit for this drink long used to alleviate flu symptoms and ward off the winter cold. Since at least the late 1700s, people have been mixing whiskey with hot water, sugar, and spices to make hot toddies, and the recipe hasn't changed much in the centuries since. That's because it's perfect just the way it is.

½ cup water
1 tablespoon honey
1½ ounces bourbon

1 lemon wedge
1 cinnamon stick

Boil the water and pour it into a mug. Give it a minute to come down from boiling and warm up the cup. Add in the honey and stir until dissolved. Pour in the bourbon. Squeeze the juice from the lemon wedge into the drink and then drop in the wedge. Stir again with the cinnamon stick and leave in as garnish.

BOURBON COCKTAILS
SAZERAC

The Sazerac was, at one point, one of those newfangled cocktails that led people to start asking for an "old-fashioned" (see page 63 for the history). That, however, was a long time ago. The Sazerac has been beloved in its birthplace of New Orleans since the 1800s. The story goes that the original Sazerac was made with Sazerac-de-Forge & Fils, a French cognac, and Peychaud's bitters that was developed by a local pharmacist for medicinal use. This likely was first developed at the Sazerac House, which was probably an importer and bar, but as with most cocktails, historical accuracy is a wobbly business.

Bartenders switched to rye when the grapevines of Europe became infested with phylloxera at the end of the nineteenth century and wine production fell off for years. Despite the switch to whiskey, the old name stuck. Today, this French Quarter favorite is often made with bourbon, which also has a long history in Louisiana, and in 2008 it was made the official cocktail of its home city of New Orleans.

1 sugar cube	absinthe or other anise liquor,
4 dashes Peychaud's bitters	to rinse
2 ounces bourbon or rye	lemon twist for garnish

Chill an old-fashioned glass. In another glass, muddle the sugar cube and bitters. Stir in the bourbon. Rinse the chilled glass with absinthe by swirling the absinthe in the glass and discarding the excess. Pour in the bourbon mixture and gently squeeze the twist over the cocktail, then place it on the rim as garnish.

TASTING NOTES

ENJOYING BOURBON

BOURBON — The Details

Brand Name

Distiller

Age

ABV/Proof

Date

State of Distillation

Price per Glass/Bottle

Tasting Location

NOSE — Choose All That Apply

SWEET
- O caramel/toffee
- O vanilla
- O honey
- O maple syrup
- O chocolate

FRUITY & FLORAL
- O apple
- O pear
- O cherry

- O berry
- O dark fruit
- O lemon
- O orange
- O grapefruit
- O rose
- O honeysuckle
- O lilac

SPICY & HERBAL
- O black pepper

- O tobacco
- O cloves
- O cinnamon sticks
- O mint
- O licorice
- O ginger

WOODY & NUTTY
- O oak
- O cedar
- O pine

- O sawdust
- O coffee
- O charcoal smoke
- O almond
- O pecan
- O hazelnut
- O walnut

OTHER
....
....

STYLE — Choose One

- O Neat
- O With Water
- O On the Rocks

COLOR — Circle One

TASTING WHEEL

Rate your tasting experience, 1 (lowest) to 5 (highest)

Tears, Caramel, Corn, Malt/Grain, Wood, Tannins, Char, Vanilla, Dark Fruit, Citrus, Flowers, Spices, Herbs, Nuts, Heat, Linger

TASTING NOTES

Describe the First Sip

....

....

....

Describe the Third Sip

....

....

....

Describe the Body and Finish

....

....

....

What Is Most Striking About This Bourbon?

....

....

....

Additional Notes

....

....

....

....

GUIDED TASTING

Write It Out

QUALITY RATING

☆ ☆ ☆ ☆ ☆

COST RATING

OVERALL RATING

RATE IT

Fill It In

ENJOYING BOURBON

BOURBON
The Details

Brand Name

Distiller

Age

ABV/Proof

Date

State of Distillation

Price per Glass/Bottle

Tasting Location

NOSE
Choose All That Apply

SWEET
- ○ caramel/toffee
- ○ vanilla
- ○ honey
- ○ maple syrup
- ○ chocolate

FRUITY & FLORAL
- ○ apple
- ○ pear
- ○ cherry

- ○ berry
- ○ dark fruit
- ○ lemon
- ○ orange
- ○ grapefruit
- ○ rose
- ○ honeysuckle
- ○ lilac

SPICY & HERBAL
- ○ black pepper

- ○ tobacco
- ○ cloves
- ○ cinnamon sticks
- ○ mint
- ○ licorice
- ○ ginger

WOODY & NUTTY
- ○ oak
- ○ cedar
- ○ pine

- ○ sawdust
- ○ coffee
- ○ charcoal smoke
- ○ almond
- ○ pecan
- ○ hazelnut
- ○ walnut

OTHER
....
....

STYLE
Choose One

- ○ Neat
- ○ With Water
- ○ On the Rocks

TASTING WHEEL

Rate your tasting experience, 1 (lowest) to 5 (highest)

COLOR
Circle One

Describe the First Sip

....

....

....

Describe the Third Sip

....

....

....

Describe the Body and Finish

....

....

....

What Is Most Striking About This Bourbon?

....

....

....

Additional Notes

....

....

....

....

GUIDED TASTING

Write It Out

QUALITY RATING

COST RATING

OVERALL RATING

RATE IT

Fill It In

BOURBON
The Details

Brand Name   Distiller

Age   ABV/Proof   Date

State of Distillation   Price per Glass/Bottle   Tasting Location

NOSE
Choose All That Apply

SWEET
- ○ caramel/toffee
- ○ vanilla
- ○ honey
- ○ maple syrup
- ○ chocolate

FRUITY & FLORAL
- ○ apple
- ○ pear
- ○ cherry

- ○ berry
- ○ dark fruit
- ○ lemon
- ○ orange
- ○ grapefruit
- ○ rose
- ○ honeysuckle
- ○ lilac

SPICY & HERBAL
- ○ black pepper

- ○ tobacco
- ○ cloves
- ○ cinnamon sticks
- ○ mint
- ○ licorice
- ○ ginger

WOODY & NUTTY
- ○ oak
- ○ cedar
- ○ pine

- ○ sawdust
- ○ coffee
- ○ charcoal smoke
- ○ almond
- ○ pecan
- ○ hazelnut
- ○ walnut

OTHER

STYLE
Choose One

- ○ Neat
- ○ With Water
- ○ On the Rocks

COLOR
Circle One

TASTING WHEEL

Rate your tasting experience, 1 (lowest) to 5 (highest)

Tears, Linger, Caramel, Heat, Corn, Nuts, Malt/Grain, Herbs, Wood, Spices, Tannins, Flowers, Char, Citrus, Dark Fruit, Vanilla

Describe the First Sip

....

....

....

Describe the Third Sip

....

....

....

Describe the Body and Finish

....

....

....

What Is Most Striking About This Bourbon?

....

....

....

Additional Notes

....

....

....

....

GUIDED TASTING

Write It Out

QUALITY RATING   **COST RATING**   **OVERALL RATING**

RATE IT

Fill It In

ENJOYING BOURBON

BOURBON
The Details

Brand Name

Distiller

Age

ABV/Proof

Date

State of Distillation

Price per Glass/Bottle

Tasting Location

NOSE
Choose All That Apply

SWEET
- ○ caramel/toffee
- ○ vanilla
- ○ honey
- ○ maple syrup
- ○ chocolate

FRUITY & FLORAL
- ○ apple
- ○ pear
- ○ cherry

- ○ berry
- ○ dark fruit
- ○ lemon
- ○ orange
- ○ grapefruit
- ○ rose
- ○ honeysuckle
- ○ lilac

SPICY & HERBAL
- ○ black pepper

- ○ tobacco
- ○ cloves
- ○ cinnamon sticks
- ○ mint
- ○ licorice
- ○ ginger

WOODY & NUTTY
- ○ oak
- ○ cedar
- ○ pine

- ○ sawdust
- ○ coffee
- ○ charcoal smoke
- ○ almond
- ○ pecan
- ○ hazelnut
- ○ walnut

OTHER
....
....

STYLE
Choose One

- ○ Neat
- ○ With Water
- ○ On the Rocks

COLOR
Circle One

TASTING WHEEL

Rate your tasting experience, 1 (lowest) to 5 (highest)

Describe the First Sip

....

....

....

Describe the Third Sip

....

....

....

Describe the Body and Finish

....

....

....

What Is Most Striking About This Bourbon?

....

....

....

Additional Notes

....

....

....

....

GUIDED TASTING

Write It Out

QUALITY RATING

☆ ☆ ☆ ☆ ☆

COST RATING

OVERALL RATING

RATE IT

Fill It In

ENJOYING BOURBON

BOURBON
The Details

Brand Name

Distiller

Age

ABV/Proof

Date

State of Distillation

Price per Glass/Bottle

Tasting Location

NOSE
Choose All That Apply

SWEET
- ○ caramel/toffee
- ○ vanilla
- ○ honey
- ○ maple syrup
- ○ chocolate

FRUITY & FLORAL
- ○ apple
- ○ pear
- ○ cherry

- ○ berry
- ○ dark fruit
- ○ lemon
- ○ orange
- ○ grapefruit
- ○ rose
- ○ honeysuckle
- ○ lilac

SPICY & HERBAL
- ○ black pepper

- ○ tobacco
- ○ cloves
- ○ cinnamon sticks
- ○ mint
- ○ licorice
- ○ ginger

WOODY & NUTTY
- ○ oak
- ○ cedar
- ○ pine

- ○ sawdust
- ○ coffee
- ○ charcoal smoke
- ○ almond
- ○ pecan
- ○ hazelnut
- ○ walnut

OTHER
....
....

STYLE
Choose One

- ○ Neat
- ○ With Water
- ○ On the Rocks

COLOR
Circle One

TASTING WHEEL

Rate your tasting experience, 1 (lowest) to 5 (highest)

Describe the First Sip

....

....

....

Describe the Third Sip

....

....

....

Describe the Body and Finish

....

....

....

What Is Most Striking About This Bourbon?

....

....

....

Additional Notes

....

....

....

....

GUIDED TASTING

Write It Out

QUALITY RATING   COST RATING   OVERALL RATING

☆ ☆ ☆ ☆ ☆

RATE IT

Fill It In

ENJOYING BOURBON

BOURBON
The Details

Brand Name .... Distiller

Age .... ABV/Proof .... Date

State of Distillation .... Price per Glass/Bottle .... Tasting Location

NOSE
Choose All That Apply

SWEET
- ○ caramel/toffee
- ○ vanilla
- ○ honey
- ○ maple syrup
- ○ chocolate

FRUITY & FLORAL
- ○ apple
- ○ pear
- ○ cherry

- ○ berry
- ○ dark fruit
- ○ lemon
- ○ orange
- ○ grapefruit
- ○ rose
- ○ honeysuckle
- ○ lilac

SPICY & HERBAL
- ○ black pepper

- ○ tobacco
- ○ cloves
- ○ cinnamon sticks
- ○ mint
- ○ licorice
- ○ ginger

WOODY & NUTTY
- ○ oak
- ○ cedar
- ○ pine

- ○ sawdust
- ○ coffee
- ○ charcoal smoke
- ○ almond
- ○ pecan
- ○ hazelnut
- ○ walnut

OTHER
....
....

STYLE
Choose One

- ○ Neat
- ○ With Water
- ○ On the Rocks

COLOR
Circle One

TASTING WHEEL

Rate your tasting experience, 1 (lowest) to 5 (highest)

Tears · Linger · Caramel · Heat · Corn · Nuts · Malt/Grain · Herbs · Wood · Spices · Tannins · Flowers · Char · Citrus · Vanilla · Dark Fruit

TASTING NOTES

Describe the First Sip

....

....

....

Describe the Third Sip

....

....

....

Describe the Body and Finish

....

....

....

What Is Most Striking About This Bourbon?

....

....

....

Additional Notes

....

....

....

....

GUIDED TASTING

Write It Out

QUALITY RATING

COST RATING

OVERALL RATING

RATE IT

Fill It In

ENJOYING BOURBON

BOURBON
The Details

Brand Name

Distiller

Age

ABV/Proof

Date

State of Distillation

Price per Glass/Bottle

Tasting Location

NOSE
Choose All That Apply

SWEET
- ○ caramel/toffee
- ○ vanilla
- ○ honey
- ○ maple syrup
- ○ chocolate

FRUITY & FLORAL
- ○ apple
- ○ pear
- ○ cherry

- ○ berry
- ○ dark fruit
- ○ lemon
- ○ orange
- ○ grapefruit
- ○ rose
- ○ honeysuckle
- ○ lilac

SPICY & HERBAL
- ○ black pepper

- ○ tobacco
- ○ cloves
- ○ cinnamon sticks
- ○ mint
- ○ licorice
- ○ ginger

WOODY & NUTTY
- ○ oak
- ○ cedar
- ○ pine

- ○ sawdust
- ○ coffee
- ○ charcoal smoke
- ○ almond
- ○ pecan
- ○ hazelnut
- ○ walnut

OTHER
....
....

STYLE
Choose One

- ○ Neat
- ○ With Water
- ○ On the Rocks

TASTING WHEEL

Rate your tasting experience, 1 (lowest) to 5 (highest)

COLOR
Circle One

Describe the First Sip

....

....

....

Describe the Third Sip

....

....

....

Describe the Body and Finish

....

....

....

What Is Most Striking About This Bourbon?

....

....

....

Additional Notes

....

....

....

....

GUIDED TASTING
Write It Out

QUALITY RATING	COST RATING	OVERALL RATING
☆☆☆☆☆		

RATE IT
Fill It In

ENJOYING BOURBON

BOURBON
The Details

Brand Name

Distiller

Age

ABV/Proof

Date

State of Distillation

Price per Glass/Bottle

Tasting Location

NOSE
Choose All That Apply

SWEET
- ○ caramel/toffee
- ○ vanilla
- ○ honey
- ○ maple syrup
- ○ chocolate

FRUITY & FLORAL
- ○ apple
- ○ pear
- ○ cherry

- ○ berry
- ○ dark fruit
- ○ lemon
- ○ orange
- ○ grapefruit
- ○ rose
- ○ honeysuckle
- ○ lilac

SPICY & HERBAL
- ○ black pepper

- ○ tobacco
- ○ cloves
- ○ cinnamon sticks
- ○ mint
- ○ licorice
- ○ ginger

WOODY & NUTTY
- ○ oak
- ○ cedar
- ○ pine

- ○ sawdust
- ○ coffee
- ○ charcoal smoke
- ○ almond
- ○ pecan
- ○ hazelnut
- ○ walnut

OTHER

STYLE
Choose One

- ○ Neat
- ○ With Water
- ○ On the Rocks

COLOR
Circle One

TASTING WHEEL

Rate your tasting experience, 1 (lowest) to 5 (highest)

Tears, Linger, Heat, Nuts, Herbs, Spices, Flowers, Citrus, Dark Fruit, Vanilla, Char, Tannins, Wood, Malt/Grain, Corn, Caramel

Describe the First Sip

....

....

....

Describe the Third Sip

....

....

....

Describe the Body and Finish

....

....

....

What Is Most Striking About This Bourbon?

....

....

....

Additional Notes

....

....

....

....

GUIDED TASTING
Write It Out

QUALITY RATING	COST RATING	OVERALL RATING

RATE IT
Fill It In

ENJOYING BOURBON

BOURBON
The Details

Brand Name

Distiller

Age

ABV/Proof

Date

State of Distillation

Price per Glass/Bottle

Tasting Location

NOSE
Choose All That Apply

SWEET
- caramel/toffee
- vanilla
- honey
- maple syrup
- chocolate

FRUITY & FLORAL
- apple
- pear
- cherry

- berry
- dark fruit
- lemon
- orange
- grapefruit
- rose
- honeysuckle
- lilac

SPICY & HERBAL
- black pepper

- tobacco
- cloves
- cinnamon sticks
- mint
- licorice
- ginger

WOODY & NUTTY
- oak
- cedar
- pine

- sawdust
- coffee
- charcoal smoke
- almond
- pecan
- hazelnut
- walnut

OTHER

STYLE
Choose One

- Neat
- With Water
- On the Rocks

COLOR
Circle One

TASTING WHEEL

Rate your tasting experience, 1 (lowest) to 5 (highest)

Tears, Caramel, Corn, Malt/Grain, Wood, Tannins, Char, Vanilla, Dark Fruit, Citrus, Flowers, Spices, Herbs, Nuts, Heat, Linger

TASTING NOTES

Describe the First Sip

....

....

....

Describe the Third Sip

....

....

....

Describe the Body and Finish

....

....

....

What Is Most Striking About This Bourbon?

....

....

....

Additional Notes

....

....

....

....

GUIDED TASTING — Write It Out

QUALITY RATING ☆☆☆☆☆ **COST RATING** ⑤⑤⑤⑤⑤ **OVERALL RATING**

RATE IT — Fill It In

ENJOYING BOURBON

BOURBON
The Details

Brand Name

Distiller

Age

ABV/Proof

Date

State of Distillation

Price per Glass/Bottle

Tasting Location

NOSE
Choose All That Apply

SWEET
- ◯ caramel/toffee
- ◯ vanilla
- ◯ honey
- ◯ maple syrup
- ◯ chocolate

FRUITY & FLORAL
- ◯ apple
- ◯ pear
- ◯ cherry

- ◯ berry
- ◯ dark fruit
- ◯ lemon
- ◯ orange
- ◯ grapefruit
- ◯ rose
- ◯ honeysuckle
- ◯ lilac

SPICY & HERBAL
- ◯ black pepper

- ◯ tobacco
- ◯ cloves
- ◯ cinnamon sticks
- ◯ mint
- ◯ licorice
- ◯ ginger

WOODY & NUTTY
- ◯ oak
- ◯ cedar
- ◯ pine

- ◯ sawdust
- ◯ coffee
- ◯ charcoal smoke
- ◯ almond
- ◯ pecan
- ◯ hazelnut
- ◯ walnut

OTHER

STYLE
Choose One

- ◯ Neat
- ◯ With Water
- ◯ On the Rocks

COLOR
Circle One

TASTING WHEEL

Rate your tasting experience, 1 (lowest) to 5 (highest)

Tears — Linger — Caramel — Heat — Corn — Nuts — Malt/Grain — Herbs — Wood — Spices — Tannins — Flowers — Char — Citrus — Vanilla — Dark Fruit

TASTING NOTES

Describe the First Sip

....

....

....

Describe the Third Sip

....

....

....

Describe the Body and Finish

....

....

....

What Is Most Striking About This Bourbon?

....

....

....

Additional Notes

....

....

....

....

GUIDED TASTING — Write It Out

QUALITY RATING

☆ ☆ ☆ ☆ ☆

COST RATING

  Ⓢ Ⓢ Ⓢ

OVERALL RATING

RATE IT — Fill It In

ENJOYING BOURBON

BOURBON
The Details

Brand Name .... Distiller

Age .... ABV/Proof .... Date

State of Distillation .... Price per Glass/Bottle .... Tasting Location

NOSE
Choose All That Apply

SWEET
- ○ caramel/toffee
- ○ vanilla
- ○ honey
- ○ maple syrup
- ○ chocolate

FRUITY & FLORAL
- ○ apple
- ○ pear
- ○ cherry

- ○ berry
- ○ dark fruit
- ○ lemon
- ○ orange
- ○ grapefruit
- ○ rose
- ○ honeysuckle
- ○ lilac

SPICY & HERBAL
- ○ black pepper

- ○ tobacco
- ○ cloves
- ○ cinnamon sticks
- ○ mint
- ○ licorice
- ○ ginger

WOODY & NUTTY
- ○ oak
- ○ cedar
- ○ pine

- ○ sawdust
- ○ coffee
- ○ charcoal smoke
- ○ almond
- ○ pecan
- ○ hazelnut
- ○ walnut

OTHER
....
....

STYLE
Choose One

- ○ Neat
- ○ With Water
- ○ On the Rocks

TASTING WHEEL

Rate your tasting experience, 1 (lowest) to 5 (highest)

Tears, Caramel, Corn, Malt/Grain, Wood, Tannins, Char, Vanilla, Dark Fruit, Citrus, Flowers, Spices, Herbs, Nuts, Heat, Linger

COLOR
Circle One

TASTING NOTES

Describe the First Sip

....

....

....

Describe the Third Sip

....

....

....

Describe the Body and Finish

....

....

....

What Is Most Striking About This Bourbon?

....

....

....

Additional Notes

....

....

....

....

Write It Out

QUALITY RATING   **COST RATING**   **OVERALL RATING**

RATE IT
Fill It In

93

BOURBON
The Details

Brand Name

Distiller

Age

ABV/Proof

Date

State of Distillation

Price per Glass/Bottle

Tasting Location

NOSE
Choose All That Apply

SWEET
- ○ caramel/toffee
- ○ vanilla
- ○ honey
- ○ maple syrup
- ○ chocolate

FRUITY & FLORAL
- ○ apple
- ○ pear
- ○ cherry

- ○ berry
- ○ dark fruit
- ○ lemon
- ○ orange
- ○ grapefruit
- ○ rose
- ○ honeysuckle
- ○ lilac

SPICY & HERBAL
- ○ black pepper

- ○ tobacco
- ○ cloves
- ○ cinnamon sticks
- ○ mint
- ○ licorice
- ○ ginger

WOODY & NUTTY
- ○ oak
- ○ cedar
- ○ pine

- ○ sawdust
- ○ coffee
- ○ charcoal smoke
- ○ almond
- ○ pecan
- ○ hazelnut
- ○ walnut

OTHER

STYLE
Choose One

○ Neat

○ With Water

○ On the Rocks

COLOR
Circle One

TASTING WHEEL

Rate your tasting experience, 1 (lowest) to 5 (highest)

Describe the First Sip

....

....

....

Describe the Third Sip

....

....

....

Describe the Body and Finish

....

....

....

What Is Most Striking About This Bourbon?

....

....

....

Additional Notes

....

....

....

....

GUIDED TASTING

Write It Out

QUALITY RATING   COST RATING   OVERALL RATING

RATE IT

Fill It In

ENJOYING BOURBON

BOURBON
The Details

Brand Name   **Distiller**

Age   **ABV/Proof**   **Date**

State of Distillation   **Price per Glass/Bottle**   **Tasting Location**

NOSE
Choose All That Apply

SWEET
- ○ caramel/toffee
- ○ vanilla
- ○ honey
- ○ maple syrup
- ○ chocolate

FRUITY & FLORAL
- ○ apple
- ○ pear
- ○ cherry

- ○ berry
- ○ dark fruit
- ○ lemon
- ○ orange
- ○ grapefruit
- ○ rose
- ○ honeysuckle
- ○ lilac

SPICY & HERBAL
- ○ black pepper

- ○ tobacco
- ○ cloves
- ○ cinnamon sticks
- ○ mint
- ○ licorice
- ○ ginger

WOODY & NUTTY
- ○ oak
- ○ cedar
- ○ pine

- ○ sawdust
- ○ coffee
- ○ charcoal smoke
- ○ almond
- ○ pecan
- ○ hazelnut
- ○ walnut

OTHER

STYLE
Choose One

- ○ Neat
- ○ With Water
- ○ On the Rocks

TASTING WHEEL

Rate your tasting experience, 1 (lowest) to 5 (highest)

Tears, Caramel, Corn, Malt/Grain, Wood, Tannins, Char, Vanilla, Dark Fruit, Citrus, Flowers, Spices, Herbs, Nuts, Heat, Linger

COLOR
Circle One

Describe the First Sip

....

....

....

Describe the Third Sip

....

....

....

Describe the Body and Finish

....

....

....

What Is Most Striking About This Bourbon?

....

....

....

Additional Notes

....

....

....

....

GUIDED TASTING

Write It Out

QUALITY RATING	COST RATING	OVERALL RATING
☆ ☆ ☆ ☆ ☆		

RATE IT

Fill It In

ENJOYING BOURBON

BOURBON
The Details

Brand Name

Distiller

Age

ABV/Proof

Date

State of Distillation

Price per Glass/Bottle

Tasting Location

NOSE
Choose All That Apply

SWEET
- ⃝ caramel/toffee
- ⃝ vanilla
- ⃝ honey
- ⃝ maple syrup
- ⃝ chocolate

FRUITY & FLORAL
- ⃝ apple
- ⃝ pear
- ⃝ cherry

- ⃝ berry
- ⃝ dark fruit
- ⃝ lemon
- ⃝ orange
- ⃝ grapefruit
- ⃝ rose
- ⃝ honeysuckle
- ⃝ lilac

SPICY & HERBAL
- ⃝ black pepper

- ⃝ tobacco
- ⃝ cloves
- ⃝ cinnamon sticks
- ⃝ mint
- ⃝ licorice
- ⃝ ginger

WOODY & NUTTY
- ⃝ oak
- ⃝ cedar
- ⃝ pine

- ⃝ sawdust
- ⃝ coffee
- ⃝ charcoal smoke
- ⃝ almond
- ⃝ pecan
- ⃝ hazelnut
- ⃝ walnut

OTHER

STYLE
Choose One

- ⃝ Neat
- ⃝ With Water
- ⃝ On the Rocks

COLOR
Circle One

TASTING WHEEL

Rate your tasting experience, 1 (lowest) to 5 (highest)

Tears · Linger · Caramel · Heat · Corn · Nuts · Malt/Grain · Herbs · Wood · Spices · Tannins · Flowers · Char · Citrus · Vanilla · Dark Fruit

Describe the First Sip

....

....

....

Describe the Third Sip

....

....

....

Describe the Body and Finish

....

....

....

What Is Most Striking About This Bourbon?

....

....

....

Additional Notes

....

....

....

....

GUIDED TASTING

Write It Out

QUALITY RATING	COST RATING	OVERALL RATING	RATE IT

Fill It In

ENJOYING BOURBON

BOURBON
The Details

Brand Name

Distiller

Age

ABV/Proof

Date

State of Distillation

Price per Glass/Bottle

Tasting Location

NOSE
Choose All That Apply

SWEET
- ○ caramel/toffee
- ○ vanilla
- ○ honey
- ○ maple syrup
- ○ chocolate

FRUITY & FLORAL
- ○ apple
- ○ pear
- ○ cherry

- ○ berry
- ○ dark fruit
- ○ lemon
- ○ orange
- ○ grapefruit
- ○ rose
- ○ honeysuckle
- ○ lilac

SPICY & HERBAL
- ○ black pepper

- ○ tobacco
- ○ cloves
- ○ cinnamon sticks
- ○ mint
- ○ licorice
- ○ ginger

WOODY & NUTTY
- ○ oak
- ○ cedar
- ○ pine

- ○ sawdust
- ○ coffee
- ○ charcoal smoke
- ○ almond
- ○ pecan
- ○ hazelnut
- ○ walnut

OTHER

STYLE
Choose One

- ○ Neat
- ○ With Water
- ○ On the Rocks

COLOR
Circle One

TASTING WHEEL

Rate your tasting experience, 1 (lowest) to 5 (highest)

TASTING NOTES

Describe the First Sip

....

....

....

Describe the Third Sip

....

....

....

Describe the Body and Finish

....

....

....

What Is Most Striking About This Bourbon?

....

....

....

Additional Notes

....

....

....

....

GUIDED TASTING

Write It Out

QUALITY RATING

COST RATING

OVERALL RATING

RATE IT

Fill It In

ENJOYING BOURBON

BOURBON
The Details

Brand Name

Distiller

Age

ABV/Proof

Date

State of Distillation

Price per Glass/Bottle

Tasting Location

NOSE
Choose All That Apply

SWEET
- ○ caramel/toffee
- ○ vanilla
- ○ honey
- ○ maple syrup
- ○ chocolate

FRUITY & FLORAL
- ○ apple
- ○ pear
- ○ cherry

- ○ berry
- ○ dark fruit
- ○ lemon
- ○ orange
- ○ grapefruit
- ○ rose
- ○ honeysuckle
- ○ lilac

SPICY & HERBAL
- ○ black pepper

- ○ tobacco
- ○ cloves
- ○ cinnamon sticks
- ○ mint
- ○ licorice
- ○ ginger

WOODY & NUTTY
- ○ oak
- ○ cedar
- ○ pine

- ○ sawdust
- ○ coffee
- ○ charcoal smoke
- ○ almond
- ○ pecan
- ○ hazelnut
- ○ walnut

OTHER
....

STYLE
Choose One

- ○ Neat
- ○ With Water
- ○ On the Rocks

COLOR
Circle One

TASTING WHEEL

Rate your tasting experience, 1 (lowest) to 5 (highest)

Tears, Caramel, Corn, Malt/Grain, Wood, Tannins, Char, Vanilla, Dark Fruit, Citrus, Flowers, Spices, Herbs, Nuts, Heat, Linger

Describe the First Sip

....

....

....

Describe the Third Sip

....

....

....

Describe the Body and Finish

....

....

....

What Is Most Striking About This Bourbon?

....

....

....

Additional Notes

....

....

....

....

GUIDED TASTING
Write It Out

QUALITY RATING

☆ ☆ ☆ ☆ ☆

COST RATING

OVERALL RATING

RATE IT
Fill It In

ENJOYING BOURBON

BOURBON
The Details

Brand Name

Distiller

Age

ABV/Proof

Date

State of Distillation

Price per Glass/Bottle

Tasting Location

NOSE
Choose All That Apply

SWEET
- ○ caramel/toffee
- ○ vanilla
- ○ honey
- ○ maple syrup
- ○ chocolate

FRUITY & FLORAL
- ○ apple
- ○ pear
- ○ cherry

- ○ berry
- ○ dark fruit
- ○ lemon
- ○ orange
- ○ grapefruit
- ○ rose
- ○ honeysuckle
- ○ lilac

SPICY & HERBAL
- ○ black pepper

- ○ tobacco
- ○ cloves
- ○ cinnamon sticks
- ○ mint
- ○ licorice
- ○ ginger

WOODY & NUTTY
- ○ oak
- ○ cedar
- ○ pine

- ○ sawdust
- ○ coffee
- ○ charcoal smoke
- ○ almond
- ○ pecan
- ○ hazelnut
- ○ walnut

OTHER
....
....

STYLE
Choose One

- ○ Neat
- ○ With Water
- ○ On the Rocks

COLOR
Circle One

TASTING WHEEL

Rate your tasting experience, 1 (lowest) to 5 (highest)

Tears, Linger, Heat, Nuts, Herbs, Spices, Flowers, Citrus, Dark Fruit, Vanilla, Char, Tannins, Wood, Malt/Grain, Corn, Caramel

Describe the First Sip

....

....

....

Describe the Third Sip

....

....

....

Describe the Body and Finish

....

....

....

What Is Most Striking About This Bourbon?

....

....

....

Additional Notes

....

....

....

....

GUIDED TASTING

Write It Out

QUALITY RATING

COST RATING

OVERALL RATING

RATE IT

Fill It In

BOURBON
The Details

....

Brand Name   **Distiller**

Age   **ABV/Proof**   **Date**

State of Distillation   **Price per Glass/Bottle**   **Tasting Location**

NOSE
Choose All That Apply

SWEET
- ○ caramel/toffee
- ○ vanilla
- ○ honey
- ○ maple syrup
- ○ chocolate

FRUITY & FLORAL
- ○ apple
- ○ pear
- ○ cherry

- ○ berry
- ○ dark fruit
- ○ lemon
- ○ orange
- ○ grapefruit
- ○ rose
- ○ honeysuckle
- ○ lilac

SPICY & HERBAL
- ○ black pepper

- ○ tobacco
- ○ cloves
- ○ cinnamon sticks
- ○ mint
- ○ licorice
- ○ ginger

WOODY & NUTTY
- ○ oak
- ○ cedar
- ○ pine

- ○ sawdust
- ○ coffee
- ○ charcoal smoke
- ○ almond
- ○ pecan
- ○ hazelnut
- ○ walnut

OTHER
....
....

STYLE
Choose One

- ○ Neat
- ○ With Water
- ○ On the Rocks

COLOR
Circle One

TASTING WHEEL

Rate your tasting experience, 1 (lowest) to 5 (highest)

Tears · Linger · Caramel · Heat · Corn · Nuts · Malt/Grain · Herbs · Wood · Spices · Tannins · Flowers · Char · Citrus · Vanilla · Dark Fruit

Describe the First Sip

....

....

....

Describe the Third Sip

....

....

....

Describe the Body and Finish

....

....

....

What Is Most Striking About This Bourbon?

....

....

....

Additional Notes

....

....

....

....

GUIDED TASTING

Write It Out

QUALITY RATING   COST RATING   OVERALL RATING

RATE IT

Fill It In

ENJOYING BOURBON

BOURBON
The Details

Brand Name   Distiller

Age   ABV/Proof   Date

State of Distillation   Price per Glass/Bottle   Tasting Location

NOSE
Choose All That Apply

SWEET
- ○ caramel/toffee
- ○ vanilla
- ○ honey
- ○ maple syrup
- ○ chocolate

FRUITY & FLORAL
- ○ apple
- ○ pear
- ○ cherry

- ○ berry
- ○ dark fruit
- ○ lemon
- ○ orange
- ○ grapefruit
- ○ rose
- ○ honeysuckle
- ○ lilac

SPICY & HERBAL
- ○ black pepper

- ○ tobacco
- ○ cloves
- ○ cinnamon sticks
- ○ mint
- ○ licorice
- ○ ginger

WOODY & NUTTY
- ○ oak
- ○ cedar
- ○ pine

- ○ sawdust
- ○ coffee
- ○ charcoal smoke
- ○ almond
- ○ pecan
- ○ hazelnut
- ○ walnut

OTHER
....
....

STYLE
Choose One

- ○ Neat
- ○ With Water
- ○ On the Rocks

TASTING WHEEL

Rate your tasting experience, 1 (lowest) to 5 (highest)

Tears, Caramel, Corn, Malt/Grain, Wood, Tannins, Char, Vanilla, Dark Fruit, Citrus, Flowers, Spices, Herbs, Nuts, Heat, Linger

COLOR
Circle One

Describe the First Sip

....

....

....

Describe the Third Sip

....

....

....

Describe the Body and Finish

....

....

....

What Is Most Striking About This Bourbon?

....

....

....

Additional Notes

....

....

....

....

GUIDED TASTING — Write It Out

QUALITY RATING	COST RATING	OVERALL RATING
☆☆☆☆☆		🍾🍾🍾🍾🍾

RATE IT — Fill It In

BOURBON
The Details

Brand Name .... Distiller ....

Age .... ABV/Proof .... Date ....

State of Distillation .... Price per Glass/Bottle .... Tasting Location ....

NOSE
Choose All That Apply

SWEET
- ○ caramel/toffee
- ○ vanilla
- ○ honey
- ○ maple syrup
- ○ chocolate

FRUITY & FLORAL
- ○ apple
- ○ pear
- ○ cherry

- ○ berry
- ○ dark fruit
- ○ lemon
- ○ orange
- ○ grapefruit
- ○ rose
- ○ honeysuckle
- ○ lilac

SPICY & HERBAL
- ○ black pepper

- ○ tobacco
- ○ cloves
- ○ cinnamon sticks
- ○ mint
- ○ licorice
- ○ ginger

WOODY & NUTTY
- ○ oak
- ○ cedar
- ○ pine

- ○ sawdust
- ○ coffee
- ○ charcoal smoke
- ○ almond
- ○ pecan
- ○ hazelnut
- ○ walnut

OTHER
....
....

STYLE
Choose One

- ○ Neat
- ○ With Water
- ○ On the Rocks

COLOR
Circle One

TASTING WHEEL
Rate your tasting experience, 1 (lowest) to 5 (highest)

Tears, Caramel, Corn, Malt/Grain, Wood, Tannins, Char, Vanilla, Dark Fruit, Citrus, Flowers, Spices, Herbs, Nuts, Heat, Linger

TASTING NOTES

Describe the First Sip

....

....

....

Describe the Third Sip

....

....

....

Describe the Body and Finish

....

....

....

What Is Most Striking About This Bourbon?

....

....

....

Additional Notes

....

....

....

....

Write It Out

GUIDED TASTING

QUALITY RATING

COST RATING

OVERALL RATING

Fill It In

RATE IT

ENJOYING BOURBON

BOURBON
The Details

Brand Name

Distiller

Age

ABV/Proof

Date

State of Distillation

Price per Glass/Bottle

Tasting Location

NOSE
Choose All That Apply

SWEET
- ○ caramel/toffee
- ○ vanilla
- ○ honey
- ○ maple syrup
- ○ chocolate

FRUITY & FLORAL
- ○ apple
- ○ pear
- ○ cherry

- ○ berry
- ○ dark fruit
- ○ lemon
- ○ orange
- ○ grapefruit
- ○ rose
- ○ honeysuckle
- ○ lilac

SPICY & HERBAL
- ○ black pepper

- ○ tobacco
- ○ cloves
- ○ cinnamon sticks
- ○ mint
- ○ licorice
- ○ ginger

WOODY & NUTTY
- ○ oak
- ○ cedar
- ○ pine

- ○ sawdust
- ○ coffee
- ○ charcoal smoke
- ○ almond
- ○ pecan
- ○ hazelnut
- ○ walnut

OTHER
....
....

STYLE
Choose One

- ○ Neat
- ○ With Water
- ○ On the Rocks

TASTING WHEEL

Rate your tasting experience, 1 (lowest) to 5 (highest)

COLOR
Circle One

TASTING NOTES

Describe the First Sip

....
....
....

Describe the Third Sip

....
....
....

Describe the Body and Finish

....
....
....

What Is Most Striking About This Bourbon?

....
....
....

Additional Notes

....
....
....
....

QUALITY RATING	COST RATING	OVERALL RATING

BOURBON
The Details

Brand Name   Distiller

Age   ABV/Proof   Date

State of Distillation   Price per Glass/Bottle   Tasting Location

NOSE
Choose All That Apply

SWEET
- ◯ caramel/toffee
- ◯ vanilla
- ◯ honey
- ◯ maple syrup
- ◯ chocolate

FRUITY & FLORAL
- ◯ apple
- ◯ pear
- ◯ cherry

- ◯ berry
- ◯ dark fruit
- ◯ lemon
- ◯ orange
- ◯ grapefruit
- ◯ rose
- ◯ honeysuckle
- ◯ lilac

SPICY & HERBAL
- ◯ black pepper

- ◯ tobacco
- ◯ cloves
- ◯ cinnamon sticks
- ◯ mint
- ◯ licorice
- ◯ ginger

WOODY & NUTTY
- ◯ oak
- ◯ cedar
- ◯ pine

- ◯ sawdust
- ◯ coffee
- ◯ charcoal smoke
- ◯ almond
- ◯ pecan
- ◯ hazelnut
- ◯ walnut

OTHER
....
....

STYLE
Choose One

- ◯ Neat
- ◯ With Water
- ◯ On the Rocks

COLOR
Circle One

TASTING WHEEL

Rate your tasting experience, 1 (lowest) to 5 (highest)

Tears, Linger, Heat, Nuts, Herbs, Spices, Flowers, Citrus, Dark Fruit, Vanilla, Char, Tannins, Wood, Malt/Grain, Corn, Caramel

TASTING NOTES

Describe the First Sip

....

....

....

Describe the Third Sip

....

....

....

Describe the Body and Finish

....

....

....

What Is Most Striking About This Bourbon?

....

....

....

Additional Notes

....

....

....

....

GUIDED TASTING

Write It Out

QUALITY RATING   **COST RATING**   **OVERALL RATING**

RATE IT

Fill It In

ENJOYING BOURBON

BOURBON
The Details

Brand Name

Distiller

Age

ABV/Proof

Date

State of Distillation

Price per Glass/Bottle

Tasting Location

NOSE
Choose All That Apply

SWEET
- ○ caramel/toffee
- ○ vanilla
- ○ honey
- ○ maple syrup
- ○ chocolate

FRUITY & FLORAL
- ○ apple
- ○ pear
- ○ cherry

- ○ berry
- ○ dark fruit
- ○ lemon
- ○ orange
- ○ grapefruit
- ○ rose
- ○ honeysuckle
- ○ lilac

SPICY & HERBAL
- ○ black pepper

- ○ tobacco
- ○ cloves
- ○ cinnamon sticks
- ○ mint
- ○ licorice
- ○ ginger

WOODY & NUTTY
- ○ oak
- ○ cedar
- ○ pine

- ○ sawdust
- ○ coffee
- ○ charcoal smoke
- ○ almond
- ○ pecan
- ○ hazelnut
- ○ walnut

OTHER

STYLE
Choose One

- ○ Neat
- ○ With Water
- ○ On the Rocks

COLOR
Circle One

TASTING WHEEL

Rate your tasting experience, 1 (lowest) to 5 (highest)

Tears, Caramel, Corn, Malt/Grain, Wood, Tannins, Char, Vanilla, Dark Fruit, Citrus, Flowers, Spices, Herbs, Nuts, Heat, Linger

Describe the First Sip

....

....

....

Describe the Third Sip

....

....

....

Describe the Body and Finish

....

....

....

What Is Most Striking About This Bourbon?

....

....

....

Additional Notes

....

....

....

....

GUIDED TASTING

Write It Out

QUALITY RATING

☆ ☆ ☆ ☆ ☆

COST RATING

OVERALL RATING

RATE IT

Fill It In

ENJOYING BOURBON

BOURBON
The Details

Brand Name

Distiller

Age

ABV/Proof

Date

State of Distillation

Price per Glass/Bottle

Tasting Location

NOSE
Choose All That Apply

SWEET
- ○ caramel/toffee
- ○ vanilla
- ○ honey
- ○ maple syrup
- ○ chocolate

FRUITY & FLORAL
- ○ apple
- ○ pear
- ○ cherry

- ○ berry
- ○ dark fruit
- ○ lemon
- ○ orange
- ○ grapefruit
- ○ rose
- ○ honeysuckle
- ○ lilac

SPICY & HERBAL
- ○ black pepper

- ○ tobacco
- ○ cloves
- ○ cinnamon sticks
- ○ mint
- ○ licorice
- ○ ginger

WOODY & NUTTY
- ○ oak
- ○ cedar
- ○ pine

- ○ sawdust
- ○ coffee
- ○ charcoal smoke
- ○ almond
- ○ pecan
- ○ hazelnut
- ○ walnut

OTHER

....

....

STYLE
Choose One

- ○ Neat
- ○ With Water
- ○ On the Rocks

COLOR
Circle One

TASTING WHEEL

Rate your tasting experience, 1 (lowest) to 5 (highest)

Describe the First Sip

....

....

....

Describe the Third Sip

....

....

....

Describe the Body and Finish

....

....

....

What Is Most Striking About This Bourbon?

....

....

....

Additional Notes

....

....

....

....

GUIDED TASTING

Write It Out

QUALITY RATING

☆ ☆ ☆ ☆ ☆

COST RATING

OVERALL RATING

RATE IT

Fill It In

ENJOYING BOURBON

BOURBON
The Details

Brand Name .... Distiller

Age .... ABV/Proof .... Date

State of Distillation .... Price per Glass/Bottle .... Tasting Location

NOSE
Choose All That Apply

SWEET
- ○ caramel/toffee
- ○ vanilla
- ○ honey
- ○ maple syrup
- ○ chocolate

FRUITY & FLORAL
- ○ apple
- ○ pear
- ○ cherry

- ○ berry
- ○ dark fruit
- ○ lemon
- ○ orange
- ○ grapefruit
- ○ rose
- ○ honeysuckle
- ○ lilac

SPICY & HERBAL
- ○ black pepper

- ○ tobacco
- ○ cloves
- ○ cinnamon sticks
- ○ mint
- ○ licorice
- ○ ginger

WOODY & NUTTY
- ○ oak
- ○ cedar
- ○ pine

- ○ sawdust
- ○ coffee
- ○ charcoal smoke
- ○ almond
- ○ pecan
- ○ hazelnut
- ○ walnut

OTHER
....
....

STYLE
Choose One

- ○ Neat
- ○ With Water
- ○ On the Rocks

COLOR
Circle One

TASTING WHEEL
Rate your tasting experience, 1 (lowest) to 5 (highest)

Describe the First Sip

....

....

....

Describe the Third Sip

....

....

....

Describe the Body and Finish

....

....

....

What Is Most Striking About This Bourbon?

....

....

....

Additional Notes

....

....

....

....

GUIDED TASTING

Write It Out

QUALITY RATING

☆ ☆ ☆ ☆ ☆

COST RATING

OVERALL RATING

RATE IT

Fill It In

ENJOYING BOURBON

BOURBON
The Details

Brand Name

Distiller

Age

ABV/Proof

Date

State of Distillation

Price per Glass/Bottle

Tasting Location

NOSE
Choose All That Apply

SWEET
- ○ caramel/toffee
- ○ vanilla
- ○ honey
- ○ maple syrup
- ○ chocolate

FRUITY & FLORAL
- ○ apple
- ○ pear
- ○ cherry

- ○ berry
- ○ dark fruit
- ○ lemon
- ○ orange
- ○ grapefruit
- ○ rose
- ○ honeysuckle
- ○ lilac

SPICY & HERBAL
- ○ black pepper

- ○ tobacco
- ○ cloves
- ○ cinnamon sticks
- ○ mint
- ○ licorice
- ○ ginger

WOODY & NUTTY
- ○ oak
- ○ cedar
- ○ pine

- ○ sawdust
- ○ coffee
- ○ charcoal smoke
- ○ almond
- ○ pecan
- ○ hazelnut
- ○ walnut

OTHER
....
....

STYLE
Choose One

- ○ Neat
- ○ With Water
- ○ On the Rocks

COLOR
Circle One

TASTING WHEEL

Rate your tasting experience, 1 (lowest) to 5 (highest)

TASTING NOTES

Describe the First Sip

....

....

....

Describe the Third Sip

....

....

....

Describe the Body and Finish

....

....

....

What Is Most Striking About This Bourbon?

....

....

....

Additional Notes

....

....

....

....

GUIDED TASTING

Write It Out

QUALITY RATING   **COST RATING**   **OVERALL RATING**

RATE IT

Fill It In

ENJOYING BOURBON

BOURBON
The Details

Brand Name

Distiller

Age

ABV/Proof

Date

State of Distillation

Price per Glass/Bottle

Tasting Location

NOSE
Choose All That Apply

SWEET
- ○ caramel/toffee
- ○ vanilla
- ○ honey
- ○ maple syrup
- ○ chocolate

FRUITY & FLORAL
- ○ apple
- ○ pear
- ○ cherry

- ○ berry
- ○ dark fruit
- ○ lemon
- ○ orange
- ○ grapefruit
- ○ rose
- ○ honeysuckle
- ○ lilac

SPICY & HERBAL
- ○ black pepper

- ○ tobacco
- ○ cloves
- ○ cinnamon sticks
- ○ mint
- ○ licorice
- ○ ginger

WOODY & NUTTY
- ○ oak
- ○ cedar
- ○ pine

- ○ sawdust
- ○ coffee
- ○ charcoal smoke
- ○ almond
- ○ pecan
- ○ hazelnut
- ○ walnut

OTHER

STYLE
Choose One

○ Neat

○ With Water

○ On the Rocks

COLOR
Circle One

TASTING WHEEL

Rate your tasting experience, 1 (lowest) to 5 (highest)

Describe the First Sip

....

....

....

Describe the Third Sip

....

....

....

Describe the Body and Finish

....

....

....

What Is Most Striking About This Bourbon?

....

....

....

Additional Notes

....

....

....

....

GUIDED TASTING

Write It Out

QUALITY RATING ☆☆☆☆☆

COST RATING

OVERALL RATING

RATE IT

Fill It In

BOURBON
The Details

....

Brand Name   **Distiller**

....

Age   **ABV/Proof**   **Date**

....

State of Distillation   **Price per Glass/Bottle**   **Tasting Location**

NOSE
Choose All That Apply

SWEET
- ○ caramel/toffee
- ○ vanilla
- ○ honey
- ○ maple syrup
- ○ chocolate

FRUITY & FLORAL
- ○ apple
- ○ pear
- ○ cherry

- ○ berry
- ○ dark fruit
- ○ lemon
- ○ orange
- ○ grapefruit
- ○ rose
- ○ honeysuckle
- ○ lilac

SPICY & HERBAL
- ○ black pepper

- ○ tobacco
- ○ cloves
- ○ cinnamon sticks
- ○ mint
- ○ licorice
- ○ ginger

WOODY & NUTTY
- ○ oak
- ○ cedar
- ○ pine

- ○ sawdust
- ○ coffee
- ○ charcoal smoke
- ○ almond
- ○ pecan
- ○ hazelnut
- ○ walnut

OTHER

....

....

STYLE
Choose One

- ○ Neat
- ○ With Water
- ○ On the Rocks

COLOR
Circle One

TASTING WHEEL

Rate your tasting experience, 1 (lowest) to 5 (highest)

Describe the First Sip

....

....

....

Describe the Third Sip

....

....

....

Describe the Body and Finish

....

....

....

What Is Most Striking About This Bourbon?

....

....

....

Additional Notes

....

....

....

....

GUIDED TASTING

Write It Out

QUALITY RATING

☆ ☆ ☆ ☆ ☆

COST RATING

  Ⓢ Ⓢ Ⓢ

OVERALL RATING

RATE IT

Fill It In

ENJOYING BOURBON

BOURBON
The Details

Brand Name   Distiller

Age   ABV/Proof   Date

State of Distillation   Price per Glass/Bottle   Tasting Location

NOSE
Choose All That Apply

SWEET
- ○ caramel/toffee
- ○ vanilla
- ○ honey
- ○ maple syrup
- ○ chocolate

FRUITY & FLORAL
- ○ apple
- ○ pear
- ○ cherry

- ○ berry
- ○ dark fruit
- ○ lemon
- ○ orange
- ○ grapefruit
- ○ rose
- ○ honeysuckle
- ○ lilac

SPICY & HERBAL
- ○ black pepper

- ○ tobacco
- ○ cloves
- ○ cinnamon sticks
- ○ mint
- ○ licorice
- ○ ginger

WOODY & NUTTY
- ○ oak
- ○ cedar
- ○ pine

- ○ sawdust
- ○ coffee
- ○ charcoal smoke
- ○ almond
- ○ pecan
- ○ hazelnut
- ○ walnut

OTHER
....
....

STYLE
Choose One

- ○ Neat
- ○ With Water
- ○ On the Rocks

TASTING WHEEL

Rate your tasting experience, 1 (lowest) to 5 (highest)

COLOR
Circle One

TASTING NOTES

Describe the First Sip

....

....

....

Describe the Third Sip

....

....

....

Describe the Body and Finish

....

....

....

What Is Most Striking About This Bourbon?

....

....

....

Additional Notes

....

....

....

....

GUIDED TASTING — Write It Out

QUALITY RATING	COST RATING	OVERALL RATING
☆ ☆ ☆ ☆ ☆	⑤ ⑤ ⑤	🍾 🍾 🍾 🍾 🍾

RATE IT — Fill It In

ENJOYING BOURBON

BOURBON
The Details

Brand Name   Distiller

Age   ABV/Proof   Date

State of Distillation   Price per Glass/Bottle   Tasting Location

NOSE
Choose All That Apply

SWEET
- ○ caramel/toffee
- ○ vanilla
- ○ honey
- ○ maple syrup
- ○ chocolate

FRUITY & FLORAL
- ○ apple
- ○ pear
- ○ cherry

- ○ berry
- ○ dark fruit
- ○ lemon
- ○ orange
- ○ grapefruit
- ○ rose
- ○ honeysuckle
- ○ lilac

SPICY & HERBAL
- ○ black pepper

- ○ tobacco
- ○ cloves
- ○ cinnamon sticks
- ○ mint
- ○ licorice
- ○ ginger

WOODY & NUTTY
- ○ oak
- ○ cedar
- ○ pine

- ○ sawdust
- ○ coffee
- ○ charcoal smoke
- ○ almond
- ○ pecan
- ○ hazelnut
- ○ walnut

OTHER
....
....

STYLE
Choose One

- ○ Neat
- ○ With Water
- ○ On the Rocks

COLOR
Circle One

TASTING WHEEL

Rate your tasting experience, 1 (lowest) to 5 (highest)

Tears · Caramel · Corn · Malt/Grain · Wood · Tannins · Char · Vanilla · Dark Fruit · Citrus · Flowers · Spices · Herbs · Nuts · Heat · Linger

TASTING NOTES

Describe the First Sip

....

....

....

Describe the Third Sip

....

....

....

Describe the Body and Finish

....

....

....

What Is Most Striking About This Bourbon?

....

....

....

Additional Notes

....

....

....

....

GUIDED TASTING

Write It Out

QUALITY RATING

☆ ☆ ☆ ☆ ☆

COST RATING

OVERALL RATING

RATE IT

Fill It In

ENJOYING BOURBON

BOURBON
The Details

Brand Name | **Distiller**

Age | **ABV/Proof** | **Date**

State of Distillation | **Price per Glass/Bottle** | **Tasting Location**

NOSE
Choose All That Apply

SWEET
- ○ caramel/toffee
- ○ vanilla
- ○ honey
- ○ maple syrup
- ○ chocolate

FRUITY & FLORAL
- ○ apple
- ○ pear
- ○ cherry

- ○ berry
- ○ dark fruit
- ○ lemon
- ○ orange
- ○ grapefruit
- ○ rose
- ○ honeysuckle
- ○ lilac

SPICY & HERBAL
- ○ black pepper

- ○ tobacco
- ○ cloves
- ○ cinnamon sticks
- ○ mint
- ○ licorice
- ○ ginger

WOODY & NUTTY
- ○ oak
- ○ cedar
- ○ pine

- ○ sawdust
- ○ coffee
- ○ charcoal smoke
- ○ almond
- ○ pecan
- ○ hazelnut
- ○ walnut

OTHER
....
....

STYLE
Choose One

- ○ Neat
- ○ With Water
- ○ On the Rocks

TASTING WHEEL

Rate your tasting experience, 1 (lowest) to 5 (highest)

Tears, Caramel, Corn, Malt/Grain, Wood, Tannins, Char, Vanilla, Dark Fruit, Citrus, Flowers, Spices, Herbs, Nuts, Heat, Linger

COLOR
Circle One

TASTING NOTES

Describe the First Sip

....

....

....

Describe the Third Sip

....

....

....

Describe the Body and Finish

....

....

....

What Is Most Striking About This Bourbon?

....

....

....

Additional Notes

....

....

....

....

GUIDED TASTING

Write It Out

QUALITY RATING   **COST RATING**   **OVERALL RATING**

RATE IT

Fill It In

ENJOYING BOURBON

BOURBON
The Details

Brand Name

Distiller

Age

ABV/Proof

Date

State of Distillation

Price per Glass/Bottle

Tasting Location

NOSE
Choose All That Apply

SWEET
O caramel/toffee
O vanilla
O honey
O maple syrup
O chocolate

FRUITY & FLORAL
O apple
O pear
O cherry

O berry
O dark fruit
O lemon
O orange
O grapefruit
O rose
O honeysuckle
O lilac

SPICY & HERBAL
O black pepper

O tobacco
O cloves
O cinnamon sticks
O mint
O licorice
O ginger

WOODY & NUTTY
O oak
O cedar
O pine

O sawdust
O coffee
O charcoal smoke
O almond
O pecan
O hazelnut
O walnut

OTHER

STYLE
Choose One

O Neat

O With Water

O On the Rocks

COLOR
Circle One

TASTING WHEEL

Rate your tasting experience, 1 (lowest) to 5 (highest)

Describe the First Sip

....

....

....

Describe the Third Sip

....

....

....

Describe the Body and Finish

....

....

....

What Is Most Striking About This Bourbon?

....

....

....

Additional Notes

....

....

....

....

GUIDED TASTING

Write It Out

QUALITY RATING

☆ ☆ ☆ ☆ ☆

COST RATING

OVERALL RATING

RATE IT

Fill It In

ENJOYING BOURBON

BOURBON — The Details

Brand Name	**Distiller**
Age	**ABV/Proof** **Date**
State of Distillation	**Price per Glass/Bottle** **Tasting Location**

NOSE — Choose All That Apply

SWEET
- ○ caramel/toffee
- ○ vanilla
- ○ honey
- ○ maple syrup
- ○ chocolate

FRUITY & FLORAL
- ○ apple
- ○ pear
- ○ cherry

- ○ berry
- ○ dark fruit
- ○ lemon
- ○ orange
- ○ grapefruit
- ○ rose
- ○ honeysuckle
- ○ lilac

SPICY & HERBAL
- ○ black pepper

- ○ tobacco
- ○ cloves
- ○ cinnamon sticks
- ○ mint
- ○ licorice
- ○ ginger

WOODY & NUTTY
- ○ oak
- ○ cedar
- ○ pine

- ○ sawdust
- ○ coffee
- ○ charcoal smoke
- ○ almond
- ○ pecan
- ○ hazelnut
- ○ walnut

OTHER
....
....

STYLE — Choose One
- ○ Neat
- ○ With Water
- ○ On the Rocks

COLOR — Circle One

TASTING WHEEL

Rate your tasting experience, 1 (lowest) to 5 (highest)

Tears · Caramel · Corn · Malt/Grain · Wood · Tannins · Char · Vanilla · Dark Fruit · Citrus · Flowers · Spices · Herbs · Nuts · Heat · Linger

Describe the First Sip

....

....

....

Describe the Third Sip

....

....

....

Describe the Body and Finish

....

....

....

What Is Most Striking About This Bourbon?

....

....

....

Additional Notes

....

....

....

....

GUIDED TASTING — Write It Out

QUALITY RATING

COST RATING

OVERALL RATING

RATE IT — Fill It In

ENJOYING BOURBON

BOURBON
The Details

Brand Name .... Distiller ....

Age .... ABV/Proof .... Date ....

State of Distillation .... Price per Glass/Bottle .... Tasting Location ....

NOSE
Choose All That Apply

SWEET
- ○ caramel/toffee
- ○ vanilla
- ○ honey
- ○ maple syrup
- ○ chocolate

FRUITY & FLORAL
- ○ apple
- ○ pear
- ○ cherry

- ○ berry
- ○ dark fruit
- ○ lemon
- ○ orange
- ○ grapefruit
- ○ rose
- ○ honeysuckle
- ○ lilac

SPICY & HERBAL
- ○ black pepper

- ○ tobacco
- ○ cloves
- ○ cinnamon sticks
- ○ mint
- ○ licorice
- ○ ginger

WOODY & NUTTY
- ○ oak
- ○ cedar
- ○ pine

- ○ sawdust
- ○ coffee
- ○ charcoal smoke
- ○ almond
- ○ pecan
- ○ hazelnut
- ○ walnut

OTHER
....
....

STYLE
Choose One

- ○ Neat
- ○ With Water
- ○ On the Rocks

TASTING WHEEL

Rate your tasting experience, 1 (lowest) to 5 (highest)

COLOR
Circle One

Describe the First Sip

....

....

....

Describe the Third Sip

....

....

....

Describe the Body and Finish

....

....

....

What Is Most Striking About This Bourbon?

....

....

....

Additional Notes

....

....

....

....

GUIDED TASTING

Write It Out

QUALITY RATING

COST RATING

OVERALL RATING

RATE IT

Fill It In

ENJOYING BOURBON

BOURBON
The Details

Brand Name

Distiller

Age

ABV/Proof

Date

State of Distillation

Price per Glass/Bottle

Tasting Location

NOSE
Choose All That Apply

SWEET
- ○ caramel/toffee
- ○ vanilla
- ○ honey
- ○ maple syrup
- ○ chocolate

FRUITY & FLORAL
- ○ apple
- ○ pear
- ○ cherry

- ○ berry
- ○ dark fruit
- ○ lemon
- ○ orange
- ○ grapefruit
- ○ rose
- ○ honeysuckle
- ○ lilac

SPICY & HERBAL
- ○ black pepper

- ○ tobacco
- ○ cloves
- ○ cinnamon sticks
- ○ mint
- ○ licorice
- ○ ginger

WOODY & NUTTY
- ○ oak
- ○ cedar
- ○ pine

- ○ sawdust
- ○ coffee
- ○ charcoal smoke
- ○ almond
- ○ pecan
- ○ hazelnut
- ○ walnut

OTHER

STYLE
Choose One

- ○ Neat
- ○ With Water
- ○ On the Rocks

COLOR
Circle One

TASTING WHEEL

Rate your tasting experience, 1 (lowest) to 5 (highest)

Describe the First Sip

....

....

....

Describe the Third Sip

....

....

....

Describe the Body and Finish

....

....

....

What Is Most Striking About This Bourbon?

....

....

....

Additional Notes

....

....

....

....

GUIDED TASTING

Write It Out

QUALITY RATING

☆ ☆ ☆ ☆ ☆

COST RATING

OVERALL RATING

RATE IT

Fill It In

ENJOYING BOURBON

BOURBON
The Details

Brand Name... Distiller

Age .... ABV/Proof .... Date

State of Distillation .... Price per Glass/Bottle .... Tasting Location

NOSE
Choose All That Apply

SWEET
- ○ caramel/toffee
- ○ vanilla
- ○ honey
- ○ maple syrup
- ○ chocolate

FRUITY & FLORAL
- ○ apple
- ○ pear
- ○ cherry

- ○ berry
- ○ dark fruit
- ○ lemon
- ○ orange
- ○ grapefruit
- ○ rose
- ○ honeysuckle
- ○ lilac

SPICY & HERBAL
- ○ black pepper

- ○ tobacco
- ○ cloves
- ○ cinnamon sticks
- ○ mint
- ○ licorice
- ○ ginger

WOODY & NUTTY
- ○ oak
- ○ cedar
- ○ pine

- ○ sawdust
- ○ coffee
- ○ charcoal smoke
- ○ almond
- ○ pecan
- ○ hazelnut
- ○ walnut

OTHER
....
....

STYLE
Choose One

- ○ Neat
- ○ With Water
- ○ On the Rocks

COLOR
Circle One

TASTING WHEEL

Rate your tasting experience, 1 (lowest) to 5 (highest)

Describe the First Sip

....

....

....

Describe the Third Sip

....

....

....

Describe the Body and Finish

....

....

....

What Is Most Striking About This Bourbon?

....

....

....

Additional Notes

....

....

....

....

GUIDED TASTING

Write It Out

QUALITY RATING   COST RATING   OVERALL RATING

RATE IT

Fill It In

BOURBON
The Details

Brand Name

Distiller

Age

ABV/Proof

Date

State of Distillation

Price per Glass/Bottle

Tasting Location

NOSE
Choose All That Apply

SWEET
- ○ caramel/toffee
- ○ vanilla
- ○ honey
- ○ maple syrup
- ○ chocolate

FRUITY & FLORAL
- ○ apple
- ○ pear
- ○ cherry

- ○ berry
- ○ dark fruit
- ○ lemon
- ○ orange
- ○ grapefruit
- ○ rose
- ○ honeysuckle
- ○ lilac

SPICY & HERBAL
- ○ black pepper

- ○ tobacco
- ○ cloves
- ○ cinnamon sticks
- ○ mint
- ○ licorice
- ○ ginger

WOODY & NUTTY
- ○ oak
- ○ cedar
- ○ pine

- ○ sawdust
- ○ coffee
- ○ charcoal smoke
- ○ almond
- ○ pecan
- ○ hazelnut
- ○ walnut

OTHER
....
....

STYLE
Choose One

- ○ Neat
- ○ With Water
- ○ On the Rocks

COLOR
Circle One

TASTING WHEEL

Rate your tasting experience, 1 (lowest) to 5 (highest)

Tears, Linger, Caramel, Heat, Corn, Nuts, Malt/Grain, Herbs, Wood, Spices, Tannins, Flowers, Char, Citrus, Vanilla, Dark Fruit

Describe the First Sip

....

....

....

Describe the Third Sip

....

....

....

Describe the Body and Finish

....

....

....

What Is Most Striking About This Bourbon?

....

....

....

Additional Notes

....

....

....

....

GUIDED TASTING

Write It Out

QUALITY RATING

☆ ☆ ☆ ☆ ☆

COST RATING

OVERALL RATING

RATE IT

Fill It In

ENJOYING BOURBON

BOURBON
The Details

Brand Name .... Distiller

Age .... ABV/Proof .... Date

State of Distillation .... Price per Glass/Bottle .... Tasting Location

NOSE
Choose All That Apply

SWEET
- ○ caramel/toffee
- ○ vanilla
- ○ honey
- ○ maple syrup
- ○ chocolate

FRUITY & FLORAL
- ○ apple
- ○ pear
- ○ cherry

- ○ berry
- ○ dark fruit
- ○ lemon
- ○ orange
- ○ grapefruit
- ○ rose
- ○ honeysuckle
- ○ lilac

SPICY & HERBAL
- ○ black pepper

- ○ tobacco
- ○ cloves
- ○ cinnamon sticks
- ○ mint
- ○ licorice
- ○ ginger

WOODY & NUTTY
- ○ oak
- ○ cedar
- ○ pine

- ○ sawdust
- ○ coffee
- ○ charcoal smoke
- ○ almond
- ○ pecan
- ○ hazelnut
- ○ walnut

OTHER
....
....

STYLE
Choose One

- ○ Neat
- ○ With Water
- ○ On the Rocks

TASTING WHEEL

Rate your tasting experience, 1 (lowest) to 5 (highest)

Tears, Caramel, Corn, Malt/Grain, Wood, Tannins, Char, Vanilla, Dark Fruit, Citrus, Flowers, Spices, Herbs, Nuts, Heat, Linger

COLOR
Circle One

Describe the First Sip

....

....

....

Describe the Third Sip

....

....

....

Describe the Body and Finish

....

....

....

What Is Most Striking About This Bourbon?

....

....

....

Additional Notes

....

....

....

....

GUIDED TASTING

Write It Out

QUALITY RATING

☆ ☆ ☆ ☆ ☆

COST RATING

OVERALL RATING

RATE IT

Fill It In

BOURBON
The Details

Brand Name .... Distiller ....

Age .... ABV/Proof .... Date ....

State of Distillation .... Price per Glass/Bottle .... Tasting Location ....

NOSE
Choose All That Apply

SWEET
- ◯ caramel/toffee
- ◯ vanilla
- ◯ honey
- ◯ maple syrup
- ◯ chocolate

FRUITY & FLORAL
- ◯ apple
- ◯ pear
- ◯ cherry

- ◯ berry
- ◯ dark fruit
- ◯ lemon
- ◯ orange
- ◯ grapefruit
- ◯ rose
- ◯ honeysuckle
- ◯ lilac

SPICY & HERBAL
- ◯ black pepper

- ◯ tobacco
- ◯ cloves
- ◯ cinnamon sticks
- ◯ mint
- ◯ licorice
- ◯ ginger

WOODY & NUTTY
- ◯ oak
- ◯ cedar
- ◯ pine

- ◯ sawdust
- ◯ coffee
- ◯ charcoal smoke
- ◯ almond
- ◯ pecan
- ◯ hazelnut
- ◯ walnut

OTHER
....
....

STYLE
Choose One

- ◯ Neat
- ◯ With Water
- ◯ On the Rocks

COLOR
Circle One

TASTING WHEEL

Rate your tasting experience, 1 (lowest) to 5 (highest)

Tears, Caramel, Corn, Malt/Grain, Wood, Tannins, Char, Vanilla, Dark Fruit, Citrus, Flowers, Spices, Herbs, Nuts, Heat, Linger

TASTING NOTES

Describe the First Sip

....

....

....

Describe the Third Sip

....

....

....

Describe the Body and Finish

....

....

....

What Is Most Striking About This Bourbon?

....

....

....

Additional Notes

....

....

....

....

GUIDED TASTING
Write It Out

QUALITY RATING

☆ ☆ ☆ ☆ ☆

COST RATING

OVERALL RATING

RATE IT
Fill It In

ENJOYING BOURBON

BOURBON
The Details

Brand Name

Distiller

Age

ABV/Proof

Date

State of Distillation

Price per Glass/Bottle

Tasting Location

NOSE
Choose All That Apply

SWEET
- ○ caramel/toffee
- ○ vanilla
- ○ honey
- ○ maple syrup
- ○ chocolate

FRUITY & FLORAL
- ○ apple
- ○ pear
- ○ cherry

- ○ berry
- ○ dark fruit
- ○ lemon
- ○ orange
- ○ grapefruit
- ○ rose
- ○ honeysuckle
- ○ lilac

SPICY & HERBAL
- ○ black pepper

- ○ tobacco
- ○ cloves
- ○ cinnamon sticks
- ○ mint
- ○ licorice
- ○ ginger

WOODY & NUTTY
- ○ oak
- ○ cedar
- ○ pine

- ○ sawdust
- ○ coffee
- ○ charcoal smoke
- ○ almond
- ○ pecan
- ○ hazelnut
- ○ walnut

OTHER

STYLE
Choose One

- ○ Neat
- ○ With Water
- ○ On the Rocks

COLOR
Circle One

TASTING WHEEL

Rate your tasting experience, 1 (lowest) to 5 (highest)

Tears · Caramel · Corn · Malt/Grain · Wood · Tannins · Char · Vanilla · Dark Fruit · Citrus · Flowers · Spices · Herbs · Nuts · Heat · Linger

TASTING NOTES

Describe the First Sip

....

....

....

Describe the Third Sip

....

....

....

Describe the Body and Finish

....

....

....

What Is Most Striking About This Bourbon?

....

....

....

Additional Notes

....

....

....

....

QUALITY RATING

COST RATING

OVERALL RATING

ENJOYING BOURBON

BOURBON
The Details

Brand Name

Distiller

Age

ABV/Proof

Date

State of Distillation

Price per Glass/Bottle

Tasting Location

NOSE
Choose All That Apply

SWEET
- ○ caramel/toffee
- ○ vanilla
- ○ honey
- ○ maple syrup
- ○ chocolate

FRUITY & FLORAL
- ○ apple
- ○ pear
- ○ cherry

- ○ berry
- ○ dark fruit
- ○ lemon
- ○ orange
- ○ grapefruit
- ○ rose
- ○ honeysuckle
- ○ lilac

SPICY & HERBAL
- ○ black pepper

- ○ tobacco
- ○ cloves
- ○ cinnamon sticks
- ○ mint
- ○ licorice
- ○ ginger

WOODY & NUTTY
- ○ oak
- ○ cedar
- ○ pine

- ○ sawdust
- ○ coffee
- ○ charcoal smoke
- ○ almond
- ○ pecan
- ○ hazelnut
- ○ walnut

OTHER

STYLE
Choose One

- ○ Neat
- ○ With Water
- ○ On the Rocks

TASTING WHEEL

Rate your tasting experience, 1 (lowest) to 5 (highest)

COLOR
Circle One

Describe the First Sip

....

....

....

Describe the Third Sip

....

....

....

Describe the Body and Finish

....

....

....

What Is Most Striking About This Bourbon?

....

....

....

Additional Notes

....

....

....

....

GUIDED TASTING
Write It Out

QUALITY RATING

☆ ☆ ☆ ☆ ☆

COST RATING

OVERALL RATING

RATE IT
Fill It In

BOURBON
The Details

Brand Name .... Distiller ....

Age .... ABV/Proof .... Date ....

State of Distillation .... Price per Glass/Bottle .... Tasting Location ....

NOSE
Choose All That Apply

SWEET
- ○ caramel/toffee
- ○ vanilla
- ○ honey
- ○ maple syrup
- ○ chocolate

FRUITY & FLORAL
- ○ apple
- ○ pear
- ○ cherry

- ○ berry
- ○ dark fruit
- ○ lemon
- ○ orange
- ○ grapefruit
- ○ rose
- ○ honeysuckle
- ○ lilac

SPICY & HERBAL
- ○ black pepper

- ○ tobacco
- ○ cloves
- ○ cinnamon sticks
- ○ mint
- ○ licorice
- ○ ginger

WOODY & NUTTY
- ○ oak
- ○ cedar
- ○ pine

- ○ sawdust
- ○ coffee
- ○ charcoal smoke
- ○ almond
- ○ pecan
- ○ hazelnut
- ○ walnut

OTHER
....
....

STYLE
Choose One

- ○ Neat
- ○ With Water
- ○ On the Rocks

COLOR
Circle One

TASTING WHEEL

Rate your tasting experience, 1 (lowest) to 5 (highest)

Tears · Caramel · Corn · Malt/Grain · Wood · Tannins · Char · Vanilla · Dark Fruit · Citrus · Flowers · Spices · Herbs · Nuts · Heat · Linger

TASTING NOTES

Describe the First Sip

....
....
....

Describe the Third Sip

....
....
....

Describe the Body and Finish

....
....
....

What Is Most Striking About This Bourbon?

....
....
....

Additional Notes

....
....
....
....

GUIDED TASTING

Write It Out

QUALITY RATING	COST RATING	OVERALL RATING
☆☆☆☆☆		

RATE IT

Fill It In

ENJOYING BOURBON

BOURBON
The Details

Brand Name

Distiller

Age

ABV/Proof

Date

State of Distillation

Price per Glass/Bottle

Tasting Location

NOSE
Choose All That Apply

SWEET
- ◯ caramel/toffee
- ◯ vanilla
- ◯ honey
- ◯ maple syrup
- ◯ chocolate

FRUITY & FLORAL
- ◯ apple
- ◯ pear
- ◯ cherry

- ◯ berry
- ◯ dark fruit
- ◯ lemon
- ◯ orange
- ◯ grapefruit
- ◯ rose
- ◯ honeysuckle
- ◯ lilac

SPICY & HERBAL
- ◯ black pepper

- ◯ tobacco
- ◯ cloves
- ◯ cinnamon sticks
- ◯ mint
- ◯ licorice
- ◯ ginger

WOODY & NUTTY
- ◯ oak
- ◯ cedar
- ◯ pine

- ◯ sawdust
- ◯ coffee
- ◯ charcoal smoke
- ◯ almond
- ◯ pecan
- ◯ hazelnut
- ◯ walnut

OTHER
....
....

STYLE
Choose One

- ◯ Neat
- ◯ With Water
- ◯ On the Rocks

COLOR
Circle One

TASTING WHEEL

Rate your tasting experience, 1 (lowest) to 5 (highest)

Tears, Linger, Caramel, Heat, Corn, Nuts, Malt/Grain, Herbs, Wood, Spices, Tannins, Flowers, Char, Citrus, Vanilla, Dark Fruit

Describe the First Sip

....

....

....

Describe the Third Sip

....

....

....

Describe the Body and Finish

....

....

....

What Is Most Striking About This Bourbon?

....

....

....

Additional Notes

....

....

....

....

GUIDED TASTING

Write It Out

QUALITY RATING   **COST RATING**   **OVERALL RATING**

☆ ☆ ☆ ☆ ☆

RATE IT

Fill It In

ENJOYING BOURBON

BOURBON
The Details

Brand Name .... Distiller ....

Age .... ABV/Proof .... Date ....

State of Distillation .... Price per Glass/Bottle .... Tasting Location ....

NOSE
Choose All That Apply

SWEET
- ◯ caramel/toffee
- ◯ vanilla
- ◯ honey
- ◯ maple syrup
- ◯ chocolate

FRUITY & FLORAL
- ◯ apple
- ◯ pear
- ◯ cherry

- ◯ berry
- ◯ dark fruit
- ◯ lemon
- ◯ orange
- ◯ grapefruit
- ◯ rose
- ◯ honeysuckle
- ◯ lilac

SPICY & HERBAL
- ◯ black pepper

- ◯ tobacco
- ◯ cloves
- ◯ cinnamon sticks
- ◯ mint
- ◯ licorice
- ◯ ginger

WOODY & NUTTY
- ◯ oak
- ◯ cedar
- ◯ pine

- ◯ sawdust
- ◯ coffee
- ◯ charcoal smoke
- ◯ almond
- ◯ pecan
- ◯ hazelnut
- ◯ walnut

OTHER
....
....

STYLE
Choose One

- ◯ Neat
- ◯ With Water
- ◯ On the Rocks

COLOR
Circle One

TASTING WHEEL

Rate your tasting experience, 1 (lowest) to 5 (highest)

Tasting wheel categories: Tears, Linger, Caramel, Heat, Corn, Nuts, Malt/Grain, Herbs, Wood, Spices, Tannins, Flowers, Char, Citrus, Vanilla, Dark Fruit

Describe the First Sip

....

....

....

Describe the Third Sip

....

....

....

Describe the Body and Finish

....

....

....

What Is Most Striking About This Bourbon?

....

....

....

Additional Notes

....

....

....

....

GUIDED TASTING — Write It Out

QUALITY RATING

☆ ☆ ☆ ☆ ☆

COST RATING

OVERALL RATING

RATE IT — Fill It In

ENJOYING BOURBON

BOURBON
The Details

Brand Name

Distiller

Age

ABV/Proof

Date

State of Distillation

Price per Glass/Bottle

Tasting Location

NOSE
Choose All That Apply

SWEET
- ○ caramel/toffee
- ○ vanilla
- ○ honey
- ○ maple syrup
- ○ chocolate

FRUITY & FLORAL
- ○ apple
- ○ pear
- ○ cherry

- ○ berry
- ○ dark fruit
- ○ lemon
- ○ orange
- ○ grapefruit
- ○ rose
- ○ honeysuckle
- ○ lilac

SPICY & HERBAL
- ○ black pepper

- ○ tobacco
- ○ cloves
- ○ cinnamon sticks
- ○ mint
- ○ licorice
- ○ ginger

WOODY & NUTTY
- ○ oak
- ○ cedar
- ○ pine

- ○ sawdust
- ○ coffee
- ○ charcoal smoke
- ○ almond
- ○ pecan
- ○ hazelnut
- ○ walnut

OTHER
....

STYLE
Choose One

- ○ Neat
- ○ With Water
- ○ On the Rocks

COLOR
Circle One

TASTING WHEEL

Rate your tasting experience, 1 (lowest) to 5 (highest)

Wheel labels: Tears, Linger, Caramel, Heat, Corn, Nuts, Malt/Grain, Herbs, Wood, Spices, Tannins, Flowers, Char, Citrus, Dark Fruit, Vanilla

TASTING NOTES

Describe the First Sip

....

....

....

Describe the Third Sip

....

....

....

Describe the Body and Finish

....

....

....

What Is Most Striking About This Bourbon?

....

....

....

Additional Notes

....

....

....

....

GUIDED TASTING

Write It Out

QUALITY RATING

☆ ☆ ☆ ☆ ☆

COST RATING

OVERALL RATING

RATE IT

Fill It In

ENJOYING BOURBON

BOURBON
The Details

Brand Name   Distiller

Age   ABV/Proof   Date

State of Distillation   Price per Glass/Bottle   Tasting Location

NOSE
Choose All That Apply

SWEET
- ○ caramel/toffee
- ○ vanilla
- ○ honey
- ○ maple syrup
- ○ chocolate

FRUITY & FLORAL
- ○ apple
- ○ pear
- ○ cherry

- ○ berry
- ○ dark fruit
- ○ lemon
- ○ orange
- ○ grapefruit
- ○ rose
- ○ honeysuckle
- ○ lilac

SPICY & HERBAL
- ○ black pepper

- ○ tobacco
- ○ cloves
- ○ cinnamon sticks
- ○ mint
- ○ licorice
- ○ ginger

WOODY & NUTTY
- ○ oak
- ○ cedar
- ○ pine

- ○ sawdust
- ○ coffee
- ○ charcoal smoke
- ○ almond
- ○ pecan
- ○ hazelnut
- ○ walnut

OTHER
....
....

STYLE
Choose One

- ○ Neat
- ○ With Water
- ○ On the Rocks

COLOR
Circle One

TASTING WHEEL

Rate your tasting experience, 1 (lowest) to 5 (highest)

Describe the First Sip

....

....

....

Describe the Third Sip

....

....

....

Describe the Body and Finish

....

....

....

What Is Most Striking About This Bourbon?

....

....

....

Additional Notes

....

....

....

....

GUIDED TASTING

Write It Out

QUALITY RATING   **COST RATING**   **OVERALL RATING**

RATE IT

Fill It In

ENJOYING BOURBON

BOURBON
The Details

Brand Name .... Distiller ....

Age .... ABV/Proof .... Date ....

State of Distillation .... Price per Glass/Bottle .... Tasting Location ....

NOSE
Choose All That Apply

SWEET
- ○ caramel/toffee
- ○ vanilla
- ○ honey
- ○ maple syrup
- ○ chocolate

FRUITY & FLORAL
- ○ apple
- ○ pear
- ○ cherry

- ○ berry
- ○ dark fruit
- ○ lemon
- ○ orange
- ○ grapefruit
- ○ rose
- ○ honeysuckle
- ○ lilac

SPICY & HERBAL
- ○ black pepper

- ○ tobacco
- ○ cloves
- ○ cinnamon sticks
- ○ mint
- ○ licorice
- ○ ginger

WOODY & NUTTY
- ○ oak
- ○ cedar
- ○ pine

- ○ sawdust
- ○ coffee
- ○ charcoal smoke
- ○ almond
- ○ pecan
- ○ hazelnut
- ○ walnut

OTHER
....
....

STYLE
Choose One

- ○ Neat
- ○ With Water
- ○ On the Rocks

COLOR
Circle One

TASTING WHEEL

Rate your tasting experience, 1 (lowest) to 5 (highest)

Tears, Caramel, Corn, Malt/Grain, Wood, Tannins, Char, Vanilla, Dark Fruit, Citrus, Flowers, Spices, Herbs, Nuts, Heat, Linger

TASTING NOTES

Describe the First Sip

....

....

....

Describe the Third Sip

....

....

....

Describe the Body and Finish

....

....

....

What Is Most Striking About This Bourbon?

....

....

....

Additional Notes

....

....

....

....

GUIDED TASTING
Write It Out

QUALITY RATING
☆☆☆☆☆

COST RATING

OVERALL RATING

RATE IT
Fill It In

ENJOYING BOURBON

BOURBON
The Details

Brand Name

Distiller

Age

ABV/Proof

Date

State of Distillation

Price per Glass/Bottle

Tasting Location

NOSE
Choose All That Apply

SWEET
- ○ caramel/toffee
- ○ vanilla
- ○ honey
- ○ maple syrup
- ○ chocolate

FRUITY & FLORAL
- ○ apple
- ○ pear
- ○ cherry

- ○ berry
- ○ dark fruit
- ○ lemon
- ○ orange
- ○ grapefruit
- ○ rose
- ○ honeysuckle
- ○ lilac

SPICY & HERBAL
- ○ black pepper

- ○ tobacco
- ○ cloves
- ○ cinnamon sticks
- ○ mint
- ○ licorice
- ○ ginger

WOODY & NUTTY
- ○ oak
- ○ cedar
- ○ pine

- ○ sawdust
- ○ coffee
- ○ charcoal smoke
- ○ almond
- ○ pecan
- ○ hazelnut
- ○ walnut

OTHER
....
....

STYLE
Choose One

- ○ Neat
- ○ With Water
- ○ On the Rocks

COLOR
Circle One

TASTING WHEEL

Rate your tasting experience, 1 (lowest) to 5 (highest)

TASTING NOTES

Describe the First Sip

....

....

....

Describe the Third Sip

....

....

....

Describe the Body and Finish

....

....

....

What Is Most Striking About This Bourbon?

....

....

....

Additional Notes

....

....

....

....

GUIDED TASTING

Write It Out

QUALITY RATING

☆ ☆ ☆ ☆ ☆

COST RATING

OVERALL RATING

RATE IT

Fill It In

ENJOYING BOURBON

BOURBON
The Details

Brand Name · Distiller

Age · ABV/Proof · · · · · · · · · · · · · · · Date

State of Distillation · · · · · · · · · · · Price per Glass/Bottle · · · · · · · · Tasting Location

NOSE
Choose All That Apply

SWEET
- ○ caramel/toffee
- ○ vanilla
- ○ honey
- ○ maple syrup
- ○ chocolate

FRUITY & FLORAL
- ○ apple
- ○ pear
- ○ cherry

- ○ berry
- ○ dark fruit
- ○ lemon
- ○ orange
- ○ grapefruit
- ○ rose
- ○ honeysuckle
- ○ lilac

SPICY & HERBAL
- ○ black pepper

- ○ tobacco
- ○ cloves
- ○ cinnamon sticks
- ○ mint
- ○ licorice
- ○ ginger

WOODY & NUTTY
- ○ oak
- ○ cedar
- ○ pine

- ○ sawdust
- ○ coffee
- ○ charcoal smoke
- ○ almond
- ○ pecan
- ○ hazelnut
- ○ walnut

OTHER
· · · · · · · · · · · · · · · · · · · ·
· · · · · · · · · · · · · · · · · · · ·

STYLE
Choose One

- ○ Neat
- ○ With Water
- ○ On the Rocks

TASTING WHEEL

Rate your tasting experience, 1 (lowest) to 5 (highest)

Tears · Linger · Caramel · Heat · Corn · Nuts · Malt/Grain · Herbs · Wood · Spices · Tannins · Flowers · Char · Citrus · Vanilla · Dark Fruit

COLOR
Circle One

TASTING NOTES

Describe the First Sip

....

....

....

Describe the Third Sip

....

....

....

Describe the Body and Finish

....

....

....

What Is Most Striking About This Bourbon?

....

....

....

Additional Notes

....

....

....

....

GUIDED TASTING

Write It Out

QUALITY RATING

COST RATING

OVERALL RATING

RATE IT

Fill It In

ENJOYING BOURBON

BOURBON
The Details

Brand Name   **Distiller**

Age   **ABV/Proof**   **Date**

State of Distillation   **Price per Glass/Bottle**   **Tasting Location**

NOSE
Choose All That Apply

SWEET
- ○ caramel/toffee
- ○ vanilla
- ○ honey
- ○ maple syrup
- ○ chocolate

FRUITY & FLORAL
- ○ apple
- ○ pear
- ○ cherry

- ○ berry
- ○ dark fruit
- ○ lemon
- ○ orange
- ○ grapefruit
- ○ rose
- ○ honeysuckle
- ○ lilac

SPICY & HERBAL
- ○ black pepper

- ○ tobacco
- ○ cloves
- ○ cinnamon sticks
- ○ mint
- ○ licorice
- ○ ginger

WOODY & NUTTY
- ○ oak
- ○ cedar
- ○ pine

- ○ sawdust
- ○ coffee
- ○ charcoal smoke
- ○ almond
- ○ pecan
- ○ hazelnut
- ○ walnut

OTHER
....
....

STYLE
Choose One

- ○ Neat
- ○ With Water
- ○ On the Rocks

TASTING WHEEL

Rate your tasting experience, 1 (lowest) to 5 (highest)

COLOR
Circle One

Describe the First Sip

....

....

....

Describe the Third Sip

....

....

....

Describe the Body and Finish

....

....

....

What Is Most Striking About This Bourbon?

....

....

....

Additional Notes

....

....

....

....

GUIDED TASTING · Write It Out

QUALITY RATING	COST RATING	OVERALL RATING
☆ ☆ ☆ ☆ ☆		

RATE IT · Fill It In

BOURBON
The Details

Brand Name ....

Distiller ....

Age ....

ABV/Proof

Date

State of Distillation

Price per Glass/Bottle

Tasting Location

NOSE
Choose All That Apply

SWEET
- ○ caramel/toffee
- ○ vanilla
- ○ honey
- ○ maple syrup
- ○ chocolate

FRUITY & FLORAL
- ○ apple
- ○ pear
- ○ cherry

- ○ berry
- ○ dark fruit
- ○ lemon
- ○ orange
- ○ grapefruit
- ○ rose
- ○ honeysuckle
- ○ lilac

SPICY & HERBAL
- ○ black pepper

- ○ tobacco
- ○ cloves
- ○ cinnamon sticks
- ○ mint
- ○ licorice
- ○ ginger

WOODY & NUTTY
- ○ oak
- ○ cedar
- ○ pine

- ○ sawdust
- ○ coffee
- ○ charcoal smoke
- ○ almond
- ○ pecan
- ○ hazelnut
- ○ walnut

OTHER
....
....

STYLE
Choose One

- ○ **Neat**
- ○ **With Water**
- ○ **On the Rocks**

COLOR
Circle One

TASTING WHEEL

Rate your tasting experience, 1 (lowest) to 5 (highest)

TASTING NOTES

GUIDED TASTING
Write It Out

Describe the First Sip

....
....
....

Describe the Third Sip

....
....
....

Describe the Body and Finish

....
....
....

What Is Most Striking About This Bourbon?

....
....
....

Additional Notes

....
....
....
....

QUALITY RATING   **COST RATING**   **OVERALL RATING**

RATE IT
Fill It In

INDEX

IMAGE CREDITS